DEFENSE AGAINST THE DEVIL

LES MORGAN

A DIVISION OF SCRIPTURE PRESS PUBLICATIONS INC.
USA CANADA ENGLAND

All Bible quotations, unless otherwise indicated, are from the *Holy Bible, New International Version,* © 1973, 1978, 1984, International Bible Society. Used by permission of Zondervan Bible Publishers. Verses marked TLB are taken from The Living Bible (TLB), © 1971, Tyndale House Publishers, Wheaton, IL 60189. Used by permission.

Library of Congress Cataloging-in-Publication Data

Morgan, Les.
  Dancing against the devil / by Les Morgan.
    p. cm.—(The Straight talk series)
  Summary: Discusses how God's power can help teenagers handle situations and issues concerning parents, dating, music, abortion, guilt, anger, and self-esteem.
  ISBN 1-56476-000-6
  1. Teenagers—Religious life. 2. Teenagers—conduct of life. 3. Morgan, Les. [1. Christian life. 2. Conduct of life. 3. Christian life.] I. Title. II. Series.
IN PROCESS
248.8′3—dc20   92-5700
                                                              CIP
                                                              AC

© 1992, SP Publications, Inc. All rights reserved.
Printed in the United States of America.

1 2 3 4 5 6 7 8 9 10 Printing/Year 96 95 94 93 92

No part of this book may be reproduced without written permission, except for brief quotations in books and critical reviews. For information write Victor Books, 1825 College Avenue, Wheaton, Illinois 60187.

Contents

Preface	5
1. It Takes Guts to Serve God	7
2. Parents—from Another Planet?	17
3. Dating, Mating, and the Act of Waiting	27
4. Should Rock Take a Roll?	46
5. Abortion: War on the Preborn	55
6. Getting a Grip on Guilt	67
7. Anchors for Anger	76
8. When Self-Esteem Grows Dim	84
9. Dealing with My Doubts	96
10. Prayer with a Punch!	103
11. Power! Power! Power!	115
12. Getting Dressed for the Dance	124
13. God Is Still Calling Champions	134

ACKNOWLEDGMENTS

I am grateful to Jane Vogel of Victor Books for her professional attitude and expertise. The privilege has been mine to have worked with such a capable person.

I also am thankful to my secretary, Jodi Sitterud, for her tireless efforts as I wrote and reworked the manuscript. Her cheerful spirit and persistence with me made the work much easier when the pulling was hardest.

As with every other book I have written, I am most indebted to my wife, Kay, who never stopped encouraging me, listening to my ideas, or thinking about concepts with me. Repeatedly, I was amazed at her willingness to give up family time so that I could write. Her reward will be greater than mine someday.

May the Lord raise up some others who dare to take the challenge to dance against the devil. The price isn't cheap, but the regrets will never come.

Preface

Throughout history, God has selected various people who dare to be different. They brought about positive changes to a negative world. While others were dancing to the beat that led to defeat, these selected ones took the challenge of moving to another cadence. Though at times the price was high, the difference they made brought hope to those that sin had knocked down low. Because of those committed to Christ, thousands have learned they no longer have to dance *with* the devil, but are free to dance *against* him!

I believe the Lord is raising up another generation to share this same liberating news. As the torch of freedom is passed to this new group, I believe we will see people released from bitterness, immoral habits, and wicked, degrading entertainment. I am convinced emotional stability will replace ungodly anger, unwarranted guilt, and low self-esteem. Because our identity will be secure in the Scriptures, people will learn the joy of prayer, fullness of the Holy Spirit, and the armor it takes to win the battle. The result: we will see the next generation challenged to also dance against the devil.

1. IT TAKES GUTS TO SERVE GOD

*T*he last thing the world needs today is another wimp. Wimps have no class. Wimps have no punch to them! They do not make an impact. Wimps lack courage and vision. They are as thrilling as having warm, limp, brown lettuce on stale crackers for supper.

That is why people with guts are exciting! They want action and thrive on the thrill. They have a lot of energy and channel that energy into daring activities. As a teen, I was no exception.

Growing up near the beaches of Fort Myers, Florida was challenging. I raced my 4 x 4 Jeep over sand dunes, dared to swim the farthest from shore in the Gulf of Mexico, and tried to get the best looking date at beach parties. There were other challenges too — starting on the football team, having the newest style in clothes, the best stereo, the latest recording, the hottest car. One particular challenge, however, was outstanding. To this day, I still can't believe I took it.

It happened while I was at the annual Edison Parade. This yearly Fort Myers festivity brings in marching bands and floats from all over America. Over 100,000 people line the streets to celebrate Thomas Edison's birthday and the fact he had spent his winters in Fort Myers. I was watching the parade with several people when my friend, Dave, hopped on his bike and said, "Watch this!" No one could believe what happened next. Dave rode right through the middle of a marching band, like a driver in the Indy 500! We were stunned at his bravery and skill. He smiled at me and said, "Go ahead, Morgan, you try it." I stood there gulping, hoping I was hearing things.

"Naw," I said. "I don't think so, not tonight."

"What's the matter?" he said. "Can't you ride?"

Someone else said, "Yeah! What's the matter? Don't you have any guts?"

That did it. I got on the bike, and when the next band marched by, I peddled to the rear of the formation. Ducking my head to avoid getting hit by a flute, trombone, or tuba, I took off. Like a rider in the Tour de France, I maneuvered to the front of the band, while they marched. Then, to challenge my friend Dave, I did a "figure 8" around the majorettes as they twirled their batons. I then returned to where my friends stood, spun out, looked at Dave, and said: "Now, who's got the guts, pal?"

My friends clapped and cheered and shouted while Dave stood there with his mouth hanging open. I was elated! However, I was quickly brought back to reality by what I saw next.

Someone across the street was waving frantically

and shouting angrily at me. As I recognized the person, I nearly fainted. It was my mom! Of all the 100,000 people at the parade, she had seen me! I soon found out she was not impressed with my riding skills, nor was she glad to know I could do better than Dave. The only thing she had to say was, "That stunt just cost you a week of restriction, young man. And you can walk to school from now on, too." Oh, well. Some people just don't know talent and guts when they see it!

The Call Remains
Today, people are challenged to prove themselves. Various groups call loud and clear. Here are some examples:

The Brains: These people carry 14 books under each arm, read the dictionary for leisure, and can make the smartest teacher break into a cold sweat. They challenge the rest of the world with their grade point averages of 5.0 on a 4.0 scale and SAT scores of 5,000,000.

The Athletes: They can throw a football 600 yards, shoot the net off the basketball hoop, run 97 m.p.h. and do 5,000 sit-ups before breakfast.

The Songbirds: This group can play three instruments at a time, sing on perfect pitch, and transform music from rag-time to rap in seconds. Meanwhile, the rest of us struggle to find the on/off button to play the radio.

The Druggies: They hold the record for drinking seven gallons of Bud Light, smoking four joints, remembering their last names and saying "wow" backwards.

The Rowdies: They look for anyone who has the guts to help burn the administration building, blow up the principal's car, and meet at the cafeteria next

Tuesday for the setting of the Guinness Book of World Records' largest food fight.

The Straights: This crowd issues a unique challenge—to be normal. They don't want trouble, interruption, or anyone to be hurt. They just want to do their extra-credit assignments, gargle with salt-water to fight colds, and have an extra library card.

The Strange People: They dare us to wear our pants inside out, listen to Led Zeppelin backward, and dye our hair green like theirs.

Electing and Disconnecting

No matter what group calls, it takes guts to respond. When we "elect" a particular group, we also "disconnect" from other groups. While that takes guts, people do it every day. I rode through the middle of a marching band, risking crashing into band members, and possibly flattening the drum major, because I wanted to be a part of something, no matter how high the price!

The same principle applies to following the Lord. It demands we evaluate what is important and worthwhile. That is why Jesus said this:

> If anyone would come after Me, he must deny himself and take up his cross daily and follow Me. For whoever wants to save his life will lose it, but whoever loses his life for me will save it.
> Luke 9:23-24

> No one who puts his hand to the plow and looks back is fit for service in the kingdom of God.
> Luke 9:62

Those choices take guts. While they are not easy to make, they are always worthwhile. Thankfully, we have several role models in Scripture who inspire us to be brave and make the right choices about how to spend our lives. Let's do a quick review of several who took the dare to serve God.

Joseph—Jolted, but Faithful

The Bible openly describes Joseph's home. His father was married to four different women at the same time, his step-brothers hated him, his step-sister was raped, and a step-brother slept with one of his father's wives. As if that wasn't bad enough, at age 17 Joseph was sold as a slave by his step-brothers, who then lied, saying he had been killed by an animal. As a slave, Joseph had to adapt to a new language, culture, customs, and strange food. Yet, he stayed true to the Lord.

His master, Potiphar, put him in charge of everything because of his honesty. Mrs. Potiphar noticed Joseph was handsome and well-built. She asked him to go to bed with her, but Joseph refused. "With me in charge," he told her, "my master does not concern himself with anything in the house; ... My master has withheld nothing from me except you, because you are his wife. How then could I do such a wicked thing and sin against God?" (Genesis 39:9).

Though she tempted him daily, he refused to sin. Result: Mrs. Potiphar screamed rape, and Joseph was placed in prison. There he met one who befriended him, but later forgot him. Yet, Joseph remained faithful to the Lord.

After interpreting Pharaoh's dream, he was placed second in charge of all Egypt. Due to a famine, his step-brothers came to Egypt for food, and Joseph recognized them. When he revealed himself to them, he forgave them and called his family to come live in Egypt where food was abundant. Because Joseph had the guts to follow the God, Israel was saved.

Josiah—A Teen King on the Move for God

Josiah was a king at age eight! Though that sounds like a dream come true, it was more of a nightmare. Second Chronicles 33 speaks of Josiah's heritage, beginning with his granddaddy, Manasseh:

> He rebuilt the high places his father Hezekiah had demolished; he also erected altars to the Baals and made Asherah poles. He bowed down to all the starry hosts and worshiped them. He built altars in the temple of the Lord, of which the Lord had said, "My name will remain in Jerusalem forever." In both courts of the temple of the Lord, he built altars to all the starry hosts. He sacrificed his sons in the fire in the Valley of Ben Hinnom, practiced sorcery, divination and witchcraft, and consulted mediums and spiritists. He did much evil in the eyes of the Lord, provoking Him to anger.
>
> 2 Chronicles 33:3-6

Josiah's dad, Amon, wasn't much better:

> Amon was twenty-two years old when he became king, and he reigned in Jerusalem two years. He did evil in the eyes of the Lord, as his father Manasseh had done.... But unlike his father Manasseh, he did not humble himself to the Lord; Amon increased his guilt. Amon's officials conspired against him and assassinated him in his palace. Then the people of the land killed all who had plotted against King Amon, and they made Josiah his son king in his place.
>
> 2 Chronicles 33:21-25

Despite such a wicked heritage, Josiah lived faithfully for the Lord at age 16. Second Chronicles 34:3-5 says he tore down the altars where people had sacrificed their children by burning them alive, hoping to appease the false gods. As a teen he was on the move for God!

After this he assigned a work crew to clean up the temple, which lay in shambles. In the process, the men found the Book of the Law of the Lord. When Josiah heard the Bible read for the first time, he was so moved, he tore his clothes and wept for the sins of his people. He then called the entire nation to hear the scrolls read publicly, and he led the people in a prayer of repentance. Though Josiah's people had been following false gods for more than seven decades, he led the entire nation to repentance. It all happened because a 16 year old made a choice and had the guts to channel his energies for God.

Mary—The Mother of Jesus

Another example of a teen who made a choice for the Lord was Mary, Jesus' mother. She was between 15 and 17 when the following occurred:

> The following month God sent the angel Gabriel to Nazareth, a village in Galilee, to a virgin, Mary, engaged to be married to a man named Joseph, a descendant of King David. Gabriel appeared to her and said, "Congratulations, favored lady! The Lord is with you!" Confused and disturbed, Mary tried to think what the angel could mean. "Don't be frightened, Mary," the angel told her, "for God has decided to wonderfully bless you! Very soon now, you will become pregnant and have a baby boy, and you are to name him 'Jesus.' He shall be very great

and shall be called the Son of God. And the Lord God shall give Him the throne of His ancestor David. And He shall reign over Israel forever; His Kingdom shall never end!" Mary asked the angel, "But how can I have a baby? I am a virgin." The angel replied, "The Holy Spirit shall come upon you, and the power of God shall overshadow you; so the baby born to you will be utterly holy—the Son of God.
Luke 1:26-35 (TLB)

Amazing! God chose a teen to bring a Savior into the world! Notice Mary's tenderness toward the things of God as the conversation closes: " 'I am the Lord's servant,' Mary answered. 'May it be to me as you have said.' Then the angel left her" (Luke 1:38).

God used Mary because her energies, decisions, goals, and purpose for living were God-centered. It took courage for Mary to follow through on this commitment, for her reputation was probably ruined. Yet, she followed the Lord, bringing our Redeemer into the world.

Other Teens Who Took the Call
While their decisions weren't always easy, Joseph, Josiah, and Mary answered the call. So did other teens in Scripture. Daniel, Shadrach, Meshach, and Abednego, though forced into slavery, even faced a fiery furnace and a den of lions, but they never budged in their walk with God. Esther could have trusted in her beauty and personal achievements as the Queen. Instead she fasted and prayed for her people, and they were spared destruction. Timothy stayed true to Christ, pastoring churches and preaching the good news. John was in his teens when Jesus called him as a disciple. He wrote four books of the

New Testament, including Revelation, which tells of the end of the world. Though only a teen when he first followed Christ, John was committed to Him until his death.

The Courage to Take the Call Today

How did these stay true and never flinch? First, they believed what they were doing was worthwhile. Second, they had the guts to go God's way even when persecuted and, in some cases, put to death! Third, they had a vision to make a difference. Fourth, they were filled with power!

How about you? Is God calling you? Are you weary of bouncing from one group to another and following aimlessly after anybody who challenges you? Why not stop ricocheting from one event to the next and take the ultimate challenge any person can receive—giving his or her total life to Christ. We can follow the brainy people, the athletes, the songbirds, or even the druggies and the "unique" people, but where does that lead? Any wimp can do that! Negative peer pressures can cause us to do stupid things, like ride a bike through a marching band. Come on! Make the courageous decision to answer God's call and channel all your energies toward Him.

I did that, and though it was scary at first, I have never regretted it once.

A Prayer for You

> Father, I want to know Thee, but my coward heart fears to give up its toys. I cannot part with them without inward bleeding, and I do not try to hide from Thee the terror of the parting. *I come trembling, but I do come.* Please root from my heart those things which I have cherished

so long and which have become a very part of my living self, so that Thou mayest enter and dwell there without rival.[1]

A.W. Tozer (emphasis mine)

Calling It Straight

1. Why don't you want to be considered a wimp?

2. Do you have a lot of energy? How do you channel it? Are you wasting your energy?

3. Review the list of different ways we label others:
   The Brains   The Athletes   The Songbirds
   The Druggies   The Rowdies   The Strange People
   The Straights

Where do you fit? Why? How did you get there?

4. Why did Joseph, Josiah, Mary, Timothy, Esther, John the Apostle, and others make an impact as teens?

5. Why would God be looking today for teens with guts? How could they make a difference?

2. PARENTS — FROM ANOTHER PLANET?

Conflicts between adolescents and authorities have been a problem since Mt. Everest was a molehill. As a teen, I had my share of conflicts with those in control. Most conflicts were minor and due to my immaturity. But the one between me and Mrs. Combe was a knock-down-drag-out free-for-all.

Mrs. Combe was a tough freshman Speech teacher. She once failed a student who, while doing a poem from memory, began to cry because of the emotions the poem triggered within her. Mrs. Combe said: "If you cannot have more control of yourself than that while giving a recitation, you need to start over!" She was very demanding, to say the least.

One day she assigned us to pronounce a list of 100 words correctly. Working through my list, I mispronounced a word so badly, she snickered under her breath. A few words later, I blundered again, and she giggled again. This time I exploded.

"Mrs. Combe!" I snapped, "I don't appreciate that. In fact, I don't like this class. And to tell you the truth, I don't like the way you dress either. Nor do I like your hair, your car, your husband, or the way you teach! Quite frankly, lady, I don't like you!" With that, I stormed out, determined never to return.

Later that day, lying on my bed thinking about what I had done, the Holy Spirit began to speak to me. Recalling the event, I knew I had overstepped my place. Before I could rest, I went to Mrs. Combe's home and asked for forgiveness. She graciously accepted my apology, and all was forgiven.

That day, I learned a big lesson about authorities, whether teachers, coaches, bosses, government officials, or even a pastor. It is not easy to follow those in authority over us, for it goes against all we hear today about being in control of our own lives. At times it is so against our nature to submit, we confuse what we hear with what we are to do. Here's an example:

> A colonel issued this directive to his executive officer:
>
> Tomorrow evening at approximately 2000 hours, Halley's Comet will be visible in this area, an event which occurs only once every 75 years. Have the men fall out in the battalion area in fatigues, and I will explain this rare phenomenon to them. In case of rain we will not be able to see anything, so assemble the men in the theatre and I will show them films of it.
>
> Executive officer to company commander:

By the order of the colonel, tomorrow at 2000 hours, Halley's Comet will appear above the battalion area. If it rains, fall the men out in fatigues; then march to the theatre where the rare phenomenon will take place, something which occurs only once every 75 years.

Company commander to lieutenant:

By the order of the colonel in fatigues at 2000 hours tomorrow evening, the phenomenal Halley's Comet will appear in the theatre. In case of rain in the battalion area, the colonel will give another order, something which occurs once every 75 years.

Lieutenant to sergeant:

Tomorrow at 2000 hours, the colonel, in fatigues, will appear in the theatre with Halley's Comet, something which happens every 75 years. If it rains, the colonel will order the comet into the battalion area.

Sergeant to squad:

When it rains tomorrow at 2000 hours, the phenomenal 75-year-old General Halley, accompanied by the colonel will drive his Comet through the battalion area theatre in fatigues.[1]

Isn't that wild? Learning to hear what is being said by those in authority is nearly a lost art. However, all of us have authorities we must learn to hear and follow. The most common authority figure in life is parents. They have a God-given responsibility and leadership over us that is to be respected. While this is not a popular message, it is true, and there are several reasons why.

Parents Have Been Teens Too

This may come as a shocker, but your parents were not born 35 years old! They have been teens too. They may not remember or admit that it was hard growing up, but believe me, they struggled too. Your parents faced temptation, failed, struggled with grades, and had their bodies go through changes. They got embarrassed, debated with their parents, and made mistakes! Some wore braces on their teeth. They all hated zits; some had friends turn against them. They got jilted in relationships, dated weird people, talked on the phone for hours, and thought some teachers were stupid. They didn't make the team every time. And—believe it or not—they fought with their parents about dating, family reunions, vacation, chores, and even music. Your parents thought *their* parents were FROM ANOTHER PLANET!

Parents—God-given Authorities

I talk to many teens every year, but never have I had to prove that parents aren't perfect to any one of them. Parents are as perfect as Godzilla is beautiful. Parents lose their keys, their wallets, and sometimes lose their cool. They forget things like dates and anniversaries. They say strange things like:

- "Do you want a spanking?" (Sure! Thought you'd never ask!)
- "I walked to school 10 miles!" (Maybe every month, but not every day.)
- "I want you to knock it off—DO YOU HEAR ME?" (Did I hear you?! People six blocks away heard you!)

While parents make mistakes, they still have a God-given place in a teen's life. Look at this:

> Everyone must submit himself to the governing authorities, for there is no authority except that which God has established. Consequently, he who rebels against the authority is rebelling against what God has instituted, and those who do so will bring judgment on themselves.
> Romans 13:1-2

> Children, obey your parents in the Lord, for this is right. "Honor your father and mother"—which is the first commandment with a promise—"that it may go well with you and that you may enjoy long life on the earth."
> Ephesians 6:1-3

The "governing authorities" in our lives are placed there by the Lord. It is as if He assigned parents and teens to each other, knowing what each needed.

When I first read these verses as a teen, I wasn't happy. The reason was obvious: My dad was a Marine sergeant in World War II and believed his three sons were his personal recruits at boot camp. He didn't have any time for foolishness, and God help the poor kid who even thought of bucking The Old Man! My mom was kind and more sensitive, but she wasn't a "push-over" either. She ran a children's day-care and knew every stunt kids try to pull on adults. So, there I was stuck between a child psychologist and an ex-Marine, and neither one was about to be manipulated. However, when I realized God gave me the parents I had, I felt better. I discovered He was not out to ruin my life or even make it miserable, but to improve it! Check it out:

> My son, keep your father's commands and do not forsake your mother's teaching. Bind them upon your heart forever; fasten them around your neck. When you walk, they will guide you; when you sleep, they will watch over you; when you awake, they will speak to you. For these commands are a lamp, this teaching is a light, and the corrections of discipline are the way to life.
>
> Proverbs 6:20-23

Parents—God's Voice

Realizing the important role my mom and dad played in my life, I began to see them differently. Though they wore clothes I wouldn't be caught dead in and drove cars that were "practical" and not "sporty," and though they thought their corny jokes were the funniest things since America's Funniest Home Videos, I saw them as God's voice to me. I discovered that as I listened to them, I listened to the Lord. When I rebelled against them, I was rebelling against the Lord. Here's the proof:

> But Samuel replied: "Does the Lord delight in burnt offerings and sacrifices as much as in obeying the voice of the Lord? To obey is better than sacrifice, and to heed is better than the fat of rams. For rebellion is like the sin of divination, and arrogance like the evil of idolatry."
>
> 1 Samuel 15:22-23

> The eye that mocks a father, that scorns obedience to a mother, will be pecked out by the raven of the valley, will be eaten by the vultures.
>
> Proverbs 30:17

20/20 Vision

Reading those two verses nearly knocked me out of my chair. "Divination" is witchcraft or demonic activity. That was the last thing I wanted! I was equally afraid of the message of Proverbs 30:17. While vultures would not literally eat out my eye, I knew that spiritually speaking, rebellion is blinding. What I wanted was 20/20 vision—Proverbs 20:20:

> If a man curses his father or mother, his lamp will be snuffed out in pitch darkness.

I saw the value of my parents despite their differences from me. It felt good knowing God gave me the parents He did so my life would be the best! As my thinking changed, I grew in the Lord. If you can believe it, I even asked my ex-Marine dad to be best man when I got married.

But What About . . . ?

Maybe you are struggling with this and are saying, "But what about. . . ?" As I have shared this with scores of teens across America at different camps and retreats, I have heard dozens of "But What About. . . ?" comments. Here is how I have responded to those typical questions:

But What About . . . My Personality? I Do Not Submit Well. I can identify, for when I am told something *has* to be a certain way, I will think of 17 reasons why it should be done differently! It may not be "natural" for you to submit, but if you are willing to humble yourself, God will do something "supernatural" for you.

Humble yourselves, therefore, under God's

mighty hand, that He may lift you up in due time. Cast all your anxiety on Him because He cares for you.

1 Peter 5:6-7

But What about . . . . My Parents Taking Advantage of Me? "Does God want me to become a doormat?" you might ask. Or you might be thinking, "You don't know my dad. His friends call him T.R.—short for Tyrannosaurus Rex! He'll milk this submission stuff for all it's worth!"

While some may take advantage at first, God never fails anyone willing to follow His way. That was true for Lorissa. When she understood her parents' role in her life, she decided to try submitting. She apologized to her parents for being harsh with them and pledged to do her best to submit to their authority. At first her dad, a non-believer, was skeptical and even took advantage of her. But Lorissa stayed true to her commitment. She baked special treats for the family, was sensitive to others at home, and even came in early from dates. She was serious toward the Lord and her parents. Because of her consistency, I had the privilege of leading her dad to Christ. He said it was a direct result of Lorissa's example.

But What about . . . If I Am Right and My Parents Are Wrong? That may happen, for parents are not perfect. In fact, I have known parents who were wrong in areas like make-up, the number of dates per month, hair length, and even pierced ears. Some parents are too restrictive, or harsh in their words, or even insensitive to the feelings of others. However, the real issue isn't who is right or wrong, but who is in charge. According to the Scripture, parents are. The only exception to this is if something leads to sin.

Parents—from Another Planet?

Otherwise, submitting to parents is the standard. God gives these promises:

> A gentle answer turns away wrath, but a harsh word stirs up anger.
>
> Proverbs 15:1

> A fool spurns his father's discipline, but whoever heeds correction shows prudence.
>
> Proverbs 15:5

> When a man's ways are pleasing to the Lord, he makes even his enemies live at peace with him.
>
> Proverbs 16:7

> The king's heart is in the hand of the Lord; He directs it like a watercourse wherever He pleases.
>
> Proverbs 21:1

While I had to sort through this as a teen, I never was sorry for submitting to the instruction of my parents. It wasn't always easy, and at times, I have to admit, I was *sure* my parents were from another planet. But as the Word took root in my heart, I was glad I had planted the seed of submission.

> Obey your leaders and submit to their authority. They keep watch over you as men who must give an account. Obey them so that their work will be a joy, not a burden, for that would be of no advantage to you.
>
> Hebrews 13:17

As we come to the end of this chapter, maybe you are beginning to see your parents differently. Perhaps you have responded to them in harsh ways and without respect, like I did to Mrs. Combe. Do yourself a favor—humble yourself and ask for forgiveness. Ask the Lord to take away the bitterness in the relationship. As you strive to honor your parents, God will honor you. There will always be someone you have to obey. The sooner you learn to obey your parents, the quicker life will be easier for you.

Calling It Straight

1. What differences are there between you and your parents? Why?

2. Have you ever talked to your parents about struggles they had as teens? What were they? Can you identify with them?

3. What key passage speaks to you about the role of parents? How can you apply this to your life?

4. Since your parents are God's voice in your life, discuss the following with them, and get their input.

Chores	Dating	Music
Grades	Respect	Church
Money	Friends	Clothes
Curfew	Reading Material	Attitude

3. Dating, Mating, and the Act of Waiting

Question: What is scary and relaxing, frustrating and fun, hard and easy, cheap and expensive, a cause for tears and the reason to laugh, awful one weekend and awesome the next?

Need a hint? It can also be sinful or spiritually rewarding. Answer: Dating!

Dating can be thrilling or chilling. For most people, the excitement of dating sends goose bumps right down to their toes, but it can also lead to a joyful kind of confusion. Here's what I mean:

    All Because You Kissed Me Goodnight

    I opened the sidewalk and walked up the door
    I slipped on the table and ran into the floor

I turned on the sandwich and bit into the light
And all of this because you kissed me good night

I walked up my teeth and brushed the stairs
I said my pajamas and put on my prayers
I knew somehow that it didn't seem right
But it happened because you kissed me goodnight

I scratched my curtains and shut my cat's head
I crawled into my slippers and took off my bed
I fluffed up my diary and wrote my pillow of light
And all of this happened because you kissed me goodnight

Now I know this is backwards and sideways and such
My tang is toungelled and I haven't said much
It may seem from this poem that I'm not very bright
But it's all your fault, because you kissed me goodnight

Author unknown

Dating is exciting for a lot of reasons but especially if you believe there is an "ideal" man or woman waiting for you. Girls spend hours "primping." Guys go to the gym to lift and grunt. However, there is no such thing as the "ultimate" man or woman.

Guys, a girl may seem attractive, but she isn't perfect. She may have hairy legs or wear cheap perfume called "Lucky Tiger." Her dad's cigar may look like a log hanging out of his mouth. (I went to pick up a girl once for a date; her mom was smoking a cigar!)

Girls, the guys aren't "picture-perfect" either. When the first picture dictionary is published, the photo for the word "stink" will be of a guy's feet. Most fellows' feet smell so bad, they could "k.o." an ox ten yards away! And sometimes they have something growing over their mouths, something called peach fuzz.

Though ideas may vary, we all have a dream of what the ideal woman or man is like. Here are some concepts and some reality.

Ideal Woman:
- She is always beautiful and cheerful.
- She could marry a movie star but only wants her man.
- Her hair never needs curlers or the beauty shop.
- Her beauty won't run in a rainstorm.
- She is never sick, just allergic to jewelry and fur coats.
- She insists that moving furniture by herself is good for her figure.
- She is an expert in cooking, cleaning, washing the car, changing the oil, painting the house, rotating tires, and keeping quiet.
- Her favorite hobbies are mowing the lawn and shoveling snow.
- She hates credit cards.
- Her favorite expression is "What can I do for you, dear?"
- She thinks her man has Einstein's brain and looks like Mr. America.
- She wants her man to go out with the boys so she can get some sewing done.
- She loves him because he is so lovable, and she is convinced she got the hunk of the school.

What He Gets:
- She speaks 140 words per minute with gusts up to 180.
- She was once a model for a totem pole.
- She is a light eater—as soon as it gets light, she starts eating.
- She tells him he has only 2 faults: everything he does and everything he says.
- Her hair resembles an explosion in a steel wool factory.

Ideal Man:
- He is a brilliant conversationalist, tall, dark, and handsome and sings like Michael Bolton.
- He is very sensitive, truly loving, and sends flowers with a blank check attached.
- He loves hard work, so his wife can add to her wardrobe daily.
- He helps by vacuuming, cleaning, and taking care of the yard.
- He has a single mission in life: to pamper his wife and serve her breakfast in bed.
- He has emotional and physical strength, as well as Visa, MasterCard, and American Express.
- He could out-think Einstein and looks like a combination of Tom Cruise and Patrick Swayze.

What She Gets:
- He always takes her to the best restaurants; someday he may take her inside.
- He never has ulcers; he just gives them.
- When he gets an idea, he can put it in a nutshell.
- He is a well-known miracle worker—it's a miracle when he works.
- He has flashes of insight and sensitivity as regularly as Halley's Comet.

- He is as coordinated as a bull in a china shop.
- He has the voice of Pee-Wee Herman and looks like a combination of Don King and Freddie Krueger.

The ideal hardly ever matches reality, and you will be surprised at all the different types of people there are to date.

21st C.Z.

One type could be called the "21st Century Zoomer!" This person wants to marry late in his or her twenties, but until then he or she wants every new fad and high tech toy known to mankind. "Commitment" is a foreign word and makes Mr./Ms. 21st C.Z. green around the gills.

Southern Style

A second kind of date is "Sam and Susie Southern," as in Sweet Southern Belle. These people are very conservative. A person must have the right "background" to spend any serious time with Sam and Susie.

It's Tradition!

In a "Tom and Teresa Traditionalist" relationship the guy calls the girl 96.4% of the time, stands up when she or her parents enter the room, and does the old yawn-during-the-movie-put-his-arm-around-her-shoulder trick. When Tom and Teresa marry, they have a lovely home with a white picket fence in front, four kids, and a station wagon with wood paneling on the side.

Supersonic!

Another kind of dating is "Sonny and Sandra Supersonic"—the wildest couple on earth. For them, life should be fast, fun, and without responsibility. They believe "curfew" is a cuss word, and that rebellion rules! According to Sonny and Sandra, standards are as relevant as a steamboat on the interstate. To them, right and wrong are as antiquated as Grandpa.

Because there are many varying ideas about dating, it is easy to become confused. We need some straight answers. Thankfully, we get upfront guidelines on how to date, how to prepare for marriage, and how to be an ideal man or woman as we look into God's Book.

Whom to Date

I've found that when the Bible speaks, the argument is over! In 2 Corinthians 6:14-18 there is no argument about relationships.

> Do not be yoked together with unbelievers. For what do righteousness and wickedness have in common? Or what fellowship can light have with darkness? What harmony is there between Christ and Belial? What does a believer have in common with an unbeliever? What agreement is there between the temple of God and idols? For we are the temple of the living God. As God has said: "I will live with them and walk among them, and I will be their God, and they will be My people." "Therefore come out from them and be separate," says the Lord. "Touch no unclean thing, and I will receive you. I will be a Father to you, and you will be My sons and daughters," says the Lord Almighty.
> 2 Corinthians 6:14-18

When I speak at camps and retreats, I almost always talk on Christian dating. Afterward, people of-

ten tell me why they as Christians date non-Christians. Here are some samples:
- But he is *so* nice!
- I've sat home long enough!
- Non-Christians have more fun.
- It's only a date!
- She accepts me for who I am.
- I was lonely.
- He's changing.
- It's my life!

But look at what Scripture says:

> The man without the Spirit does not accept the things that come from the Spirit of God, for they are foolishness to him, and he cannot understand them, because they are spiritually discerned.
>
> 1 Corinthians 2:14

When I first shared this with Debbie, she said she was only dating Tim, a non-believer, because she wanted to show him the difference Christ made in her life. Though that sounded noble, I reminded her of the next few verses.

> Since we have these promises, dear friends, let us purify ourselves from everything that contaminates body and spirit, perfecting holiness out of reverence for God.
>
> 2 Corinthians 7:1

Debbie sought forgiveness for violating the Scripture and prayed that Tim would see that her love for the Lord was stronger than anything else in her life.

Though confused about why Debbie could no longer see him, Tim kept coming to church. One Sunday the pastor gave an invitation for people to make a commitment to Christ and *Tim* was the first to respond! He later told Deb that her love for Jesus helped to draw him to Christ. Deb was glad she had listened to the teaching of Scripture about dating. Unfortunately, Joy wasn't so insightful.

Joy started dating John, a guy from college. He had a bad reputation, but Joy saw him as needing "love" and wanted to "mother" him with kindness. Her kindness backfired. Within four months, she was pregnant. Today she is living with the consequence of rejecting God's truth.

According to Scripture, believers should date believers. But there is more.

Parental Green-Light

According to the Scriptures, the ideal man or woman will see parents like a traffic light—green means go, yellow means caution, and red requires a complete stop. Parental disapproval of a dating relationship should be the voice of God to a teen.

For me, that was hard to hear. I felt intelligent enough to pick my own dates. After all, I was 16! But when I brought Tammy to meet my parents, I noticed a difference in my mom. After I took Tammy home that night, I asked my mom what was wrong. I will never forget her words: "Stay away from her, Les. She's trouble." Offended by the harsh judgment, I went off to my room for the night. But when I found this passage, I was stunned.

> My son, keep your father's commands and do not forsake your mother's teaching. Bind them upon your heart forever; fasten them around your neck. When you walk, they will guide; when you sleep, they will watch over you; when

you awake, they will speak to you. For these
commands are a lamp, this teaching is a light,
and the corrections of discipline are the way to
life, keeping you from the immoral woman,
from the smooth tongue of the wayward wife.
Do not lust in your heart after her beauty or let
her captivate you with her eyes, for the prostitute reduces you to a loaf of bread, and the
adulteress preys upon your very life. Can a man
scoop fire into his lap without his clothes being
burned? Can a man walk on hot coals without
his feet being scorched?
> Proverbs 6:20-28

My mom was right about Tammy, and I soon
stopped seeing her. It was as if the Lord gave my
mom a built-in radar that flashed a red light. Listening to her helped tremendously.

Character! Not Characters!
How you date reflects who you are. Respecting yourself frees you to develop godly relationships that have
character. Having character is different from being a
"character."

> Better a poor man whose walk is blameless
than a fool whose lips are perverse. It is not
good to have zeal without knowledge, nor to be
hasty and miss the way. A man's own folly ruins
his life, yet his heart rages against the Lord.
> Proverbs 19:1-3

The "fool" is a character who lacks a teachable
spirit, is bent toward his/her own selfish pleasures.
Foolish "characters" are greedy and draining, taking
what they can get and then discarding people like an

old beer can. Who needs that?

A person with character, however, is not absorbed in his or her own agenda. He/She has compassion for others. They respect themselves and honor others, allowing people to become what God wants them to be. They aren't cocky, but assuring. They have discipline and a teachable spirit and want to follow God's ways. When they are wrong, they can admit it and get on with life. Those are the ones to date!

Ken learned that lesson dating Julia. Julia was never really satisfied with anything. At first Ken felt inadequate, but he noticed nothing pleased Julia. Her parents, friends, family, her mom's cooking, her teachers—nothing was good enough. Basically, Julia had an attitude that said: "The world owes me happiness." Ken decided to dissolve the relationship and wait for a girl who wasn't so self-centered.

The Godly People

It is also God's plan for us to date those who promote godliness. Just look at this:

> It is God's will that you should be sanctified: that you should avoid sexual immorality; that each of you should learn to control his own body in a way that is holy and honorable, not in passionate lust like the heathen, who do not know God; and that in this matter no one should wrong his brother or take advantage of him. The Lord will punish men for all such sins, as we have already told you and warned you. For God did not call us to be impure, but to live a holy life.
>
> 1 Thessalonians 4:3-7

Flee from sexual immorality. All other sins a

man commits are outside his body, but he who sins sexually sins against his own body.

1 Corinthians 6:18

Be imitators of God, therefore, as dearly loved children and live a life of love, just as Christ loved us and gave Himself up for us as a fragrant offering and sacrifice to God. But among you there must not be even a hint of sexual immorality, or of any kind of impurity, or of greed, because these are improper for God's holy people. Nor should there be obscenity, foolish talk or course joking, which are out of place, but rather thanksgiving. . . . Therefore do not be partners with them.

Ephesians 5:1-4, 7

God's standards are loud and clear. The mandate is to stay clear of anyone who promotes ungodliness. That includes coarse joking, immorality, obscenity, or even foolish talk.

When Jan first heard this, she was a little puzzled. "This is the 90s! What should we do? Sit around and look at each other?" Thankfully, there is a lot more to do on a date than to sin or get bored. Here are some ideas:

Sports Dates: Play tennis, golf, basketball, racquetball, or even horseshoes. Go bowling, skating, jogging, swimming, or play frisbee.

Nature Dates: Go canoeing, sailing, hiking, fishing, mountain climbing, biking, horseback riding, or walking on the beach. Visit a zoo or wildlife sanctuary.

A Creative Touch: Pick your date up early. Take your

date to a place to watch the sunrise. Afterward, go for breakfast.

Crazy Dates:
- Go for a hay ride.
- Go for an airplane ride.
- Go on a double date with parents. (TRY IT!)
- Go on a group date in a convertible.
- Have a water pistol fight.
- Have a water balloon fight.
- Learn to drive a stick shift.
- Make a video.
- Plant a garden.
- Browse at a fleamarket.
- Have a picnic with other friends.
- Dress up (like the '50s) and get photographed.
- Have scavenger hunts with a polaroid camera or a tape recorder (Have two couples participate, each thinking up items for the other to look for.)
- Go to a fair.

Advantages:
Memorable
Creative
Fun
Can involve others

Disadvantages:
The date might be a flop.
Some people might think you are weird.

A Creative Touch:
Kidnap your date and take her on a long ride. End up at a studio where you can get photographed in Old West costumes. (Let her parents in on your plans ahead of time.)

Dating, Mating, and the Act of Waiting

Inexpensive Dates
- Go to a library.
- Go to a playground.
- Go to an ice cream shop.
- Go get a Coke and talk.
- Go to a pet shop.
- Go caroling.
- Go window shopping.
- Go for walks.
- Build something (models, etc.).
- Build a snowman.
- Babysit.
- Look at Christmas lights.
- Put a puzzle together.
- Walk around the mall.
- Look through old pictures.
- Play charades with friends.
- Play TV video games.
- Play table games.
- Play hide and seek.
- Play the guitar.
- Make candy.
- Make popcorn.
- Go for a bike ride.
- Sing together.
- Bake cookies.
- Wash her dog.
- Watch home movies.
- Have a snowball fight.
- Roast marshmallows.
- Fly paper airplanes.
- Ride the city's transit to park, zoo, etc. or just ride around a while.

Advantages:
Cheap
Fun
Variety

Disadvantages:
Your date may not feel "extra special."

A Creative Touch:
Plan with your date how the two of you can go out for less than one dollar and go no more than one mile from her house.

Performing Arts Dates:
Opera   Plays
Ballet   Orchestra

Musicals	Dinner Theaters
Museums	Concerts
Art Festivals	Craft Shows

Advantages:
Learning experience
Variety[1]

The Act of Waiting

Waiting sure beats sinning. God doesn't say not to become involved sexually because He hates fun, but so that life can be lived to the max! He never planned for people to be plagued with guilt, disease, heartache, embarrassment, or sadness from sexual misconduct. He wants people to enjoy the special gift of sex, but within the context of marriage. I have talked with many people who wish they had waited until marriage to have sexual relations. Yet, I have *never* met a couple who waited and regretted it.

A Special Gift

Sex outside of marriage is like bringing a roaring lawn mower inside a beautiful living room. It is not that the lawn mower is bad or that sex is bad: it is that both would be out of place. Not waiting for marriage would also be like buying ten pieces of jewelry exactly alike, giving nine of them to people who mean a great deal to you. However, you save the last piece of the special jewelry for your mate as a wedding gift on your wedding night. What would be special about that? Wouldn't it be more awesome to be able to say, "Sweetheart, I've saved myself for you. I have respected you and the Lord, who has allowed us to be married. I am yours. It is my gift of love just for you."

Honoring the Lord this way is worth the discipline,

Dating, Mating, and the Act of Waiting

but it isn't always easy. The sexual pressure today is stronger than ever. We need a strategy that will help us to win. Here are some ideas:

I can really turn you on.
REPLY: *The only thing that needs to be turned on in here are the lights.*

Want to go upstairs and check out my new waterbed?
REPLY: *Nope—I don't swim.*

Want to go to bed?
REPLY: *No, thanks. I just got up.*

You don't want people to think you're not a man (woman), do you?
REPLY: *Having sex doesn't prove a person is a man (woman). My dog has sex, and he's not a man.*

Don't worry. I'll use protection.
REPLY: *You're going to need protection if you don't leave me alone.*

Would you like to get in the back seat?
REPLY: *No, I'd rather sit up here with you.*

I do it with all my girlfriends.
REPLY: *Well, I guess I won't be your girlfriend.*

Kissing turns me on, and it's not enough.
REPLY: *Well, it's enough for me.*

You mean you're still a virgin? What are you, frigid?
REPLY: *No, I'm smart.*

Sex makes you have a good complexion.
REPLY: *I'd rather use make-up then.*

We had sex once before, so what's the problem now?
REPLY: *I have a right to change my mind. I've decided to wait.*

Don't you want to try it to see what it's like?
REPLY: *What is this? Some kind of commercial ad? Try it; you'll like it! I do plan to try it with my husband (wife).*

If you want to be popular with the kids at school, you'll do it.
REPLY: *I don't have to depend on sex to be popular. I have more to offer than that. People like you because of the kind of person you are and the kind of character you have.*

You've gotten me all excited. If you love me, you'll prove it.
REPLY: *Having sex doesn't prove you're in love. I have too much self-respect to get sexually involved before I'm ready for it. I've decided to wait.*

If you care about me, you'll have sex with me.
REPLY: *Because I care about you, I want to wait.*
REPLY: *There are many ways to show someone you care.*

Sex will cause our love to grow.
REPLY: *Yes, but into what?*[2]

Perhaps you have already violated God's laws. It is easy to do, for by nature we have a capacity to sin. Maybe you have believed some of the lies society promotes like: "If it feels good, do it." "No one is waiting for marriage anymore." "Just take the pill—you'll be safe." "Homosexuality, Lesbianism, Bisexuality are alternatives." "Have sex if you love someone." "Sex outside of marriage is OK so long as no one gets hurts." "Express yourself, be liberated and let 'er rip!" The result is you feel trashed and worthless.

Good News for Bad Decisions
First: if you have accepted one of these lies, there is forgiveness for any of the bad decisions you have made in dating.

> Do you not know that the wicked will not inherit the kingdom of God? Do not be deceived: Neither the sexually immoral nor idolaters nor adulterers nor male prostitutes nor homosexual offenders nor thieves nor the greedy nor drunkards nor swindlers will inherit the kingdom of God. And that is what some of you were. But you were washed, you were sanctified, you were justified in the name of the Lord Jesus Christ and by the Spirit of our God.
> 1 Corinthians 6:9-11

> Do you not know that your body is a temple of the Holy Spirit, who is in you, whom you have received from God? You are not your own; you were bought at a price. Therefore honor God with your body.
> 1 Corinthians 6:19-20

Second, you don't have to be chained to the past. Restoration and a new beginning are yours for the asking.

> But if we walk in the light, as He is in the light, we have fellowship with one another, and the blood of Jesus, His son, purifies us from all

sin. . . . If we confess our sins, He is faithful and just and will forgive us our sins and purify us from all unrighteousness.

1 John 1:7, 9

Third, you don't have to continue in the same pattern. Notice what Jesus said to a woman caught in adultery:

When they kept on questioning Him, He straightened up and said to them, "If any one of you is without sin, let him be the first to throw a stone at her." Again He stooped down and wrote on the ground. At this, those who heard began to go away one at a time, the older ones first, until only Jesus was left, with the woman still standing there. Jesus straightened up and asked her, "Woman, where are they? Has no one condemned you?" "No one, Sir," she said. "Then neither do I condemn you," Jesus declared. "Go now and leave your life of sin."

John 8:7-11

I met Karen while speaking at a retreat in California. She was 14 but looked 18 and had slept with more college boys than she could count. She had even posed nude for pictures. As we talked she wept, wondering if she could ever be forgiven. I shared this passage with Karen, but wasn't sure if I was connecting. We prayed briefly and went to our separate cabins.

The next day Karen looked so different I hardly recognized her. She had read John 8:7-11 again, and the Lord began a change in her. Today Karen is released from evil and is serving the Lord in her dating. You too can know that same joy.

An Affirmation

Maybe making a slogan will help you. Here are some suggestions:
- Jesus controls my dating life.
- I date differently!
- I am the property of Jesus Christ!
- My body belongs to God.
- God's ways are best.

Go for it! I promise—you will be God's ideal man or ideal woman.

Calling It Straight

1. Of the four styles of dating (21st C.Z., Southern, Traditionalist, or Supersonic), which fits you? Why?

2. How does your dating match up with Scripture?

3. In the space below, list the four principles given for Christian dating.
   A. _____
   B. _____
   C. _____
   D. _____
   What needs attention in your dating life?

4. What would you say to someone who has broken God's law about purity?

5. Using a 3 x 5 card, make a slogan from the list mentioned at the end of the chapter (or make up your own). Place it where you will see it regularly. Call someone and tell them about your decision to change your dating relationships.

4. Should Rock Take a Roll?

*E*ver heard this at your house?
- "Turn that stereo down!"
- "That's music? In my day that wouldn't be heard at a dogfight!"
- "What are they screaming for? Why don't they just sing?"
- "If you keep listening to that so loudly, you'll be deaf before you're 30!"
- "That's a Christian song? Sure is different than George Beverly Shea!"

Nothing is a more potentially explosive subject between you and your parents than music. Families debate over this issue more than any other. Music is very personal to you. Most of today's music is written to appeal to a teen. It is fast, fun, and different from any other generation's. Also, today's music expresses how people are relating to themselves, to others, and the world. Because we are living in a world different than any other time in history, the music is expressed differently as well.

Music can relax us or get us emotionally fired up. It is like a language all its own, giving us an avenue of communication without words. It can even help us memorize something like our "ABCs" or long passages of Scripture. Music also helps us to worship and helps us open our spirit to God's Spirit. Imagine how boring our faith would be without those great tunes to sing!

Because music is such a part of life, we need to know how to interact with it. No matter what style — rock, rap, country, Christian, or even classical — we need guidelines to judge what is good and what needs to go in the dumpster. That is why it is good to consult the Scripture to make the best choices about music.

Most of the 150 Psalms originally were musical pieces. Several writers of the Scripture composed music also. For example, Solomon, who wrote most of the Book of Proverbs, also wrote 1,005 songs! David wrote several dozen songs which have been preserved in the Psalms. And the Bible certainly has a lot to say about how we are to live our lives and make our choices from what the world has to offer. The Bible is a reliable source when we're talking about the music we listen to.

Before discussing this highly controversial subject, a couple of things need to be said. First, you have to decide if you want to be a growing Christian or if you will settle for a Christian life that is mediocre. I still have to address this question myself when making choices about music. Second, the following illustrations are not designed to be a personal attack, but I do have a genuine concern. I believe Christian young people want to do what is honorable. Hopefully, reading what I have to say will spark a good, thought-provoking discussion sometime with your parents or your friends. Third, after evaluating music as a listener and a musician, I have found music can be placed in one of four categories:

1. The music may be great, but the message isn't worth the powder to blow it off the page.
2. The message is good, but the music is awful.
3. Both the music and the message are great.
4. Both stink!

Using these categories, let's evaluate the music that's around today.

What's Happening Today?

Unfortunately, perverted men pervert wholesome things. And the results are always wicked. Here are some examples:

- AC/DC—They have an "S" symbol on every album, symbolizing that they align themselves with satanic practices. On their album *Back in Black* they sing "Highway to Hell," "Hell's Bells," and "Let Me Put My Love Into You."

- Aerosmith—On the album *Get Your Wings*, the song "Walk This Way" played backward says "Hail Satan."

- Alice Cooper—During concerts, he hacks dolls to pieces, suggests sex with a snake, sings "I love the dead," (referring to sexual acts with the dead), and hangs himself. Cooper is homosexual.

- Blue Oyster Cult—All albums have the satanic cross, the album *Some Enchanted Evening* has the song, "Don't Fear the Reaper," which speaks of a teen love/suicide pact.

Should Rock Take a Roll? 49

- Blondie—Debbie Harry of the group said: "The main ingredients in rock are sex, good stage show and sassy music.... Rock and roll and sex are synonymous."

- David Bowie—"Rock has always been the devil's music."

- Eric Clapton—His album, *In the Presence of the Lord* had an under-the-counter cover of a girl nude from the waist up. The number one hit off the album was the song, "Cocaine."

- The Eagles—All the group members are also members of the First Church of Satan in California. They have produced such songs as, "Good Day in Hell," "Witchy Woman," and "Hotel California," a song about the Church of Satan.

- Jimi Hendrix—He was a "general" in the early rock and roll era, but his life was snuffed out due to an overdose of drugs. He died in his own vomit. Before he died, he said, "Music is a spiritual thing. You can hypnotize people with music. At their weakest point you can punch into their subconscious what you want to say."

- Kiss—Their group name stands for "Knights in Satan's Service." All of their albums have the satanic "S" inscribed on them. In their concerts, they have been known to breathe fire, levitate instruments, and regurgitate blood.

- Led Zepplin—The album *Houses of the Holy* has a naked man holding up a child in sacrifice to mysterious light. Perhaps the group's most famous song, "Stairway to Heaven" played backward, says, "Oh, he is my prince, Satan ... the one who lit the night, lord, you made me shout in glory to Satan."

- Ted Nugent—He calls his music "combat music." "Rock," he says, "is the perfect primal method of releasing our violent instincts. I'd love to rape an audience. They are the lowest form of human existence. When you listen to my music, I hope you throw up."

- Madonna—When asked why she wears a cross with Christ on it, she said, "I think it is sexy to have a naked man on me at all times."[1]

There are dozens of other groups like these, including 2 live Crew, Def Leppard, House of Lords, Beastie Boys, Venom, Slayer, Skid Row, Guns & Roses, Public Enemy, Megadeath, Metallica, WASP, Poison, The Dead Kennedys, Ratt, Judas Priest, and Motley Crew. Some key people in the music business include individuals like John Cougar Mellencamp, Ozzy Osborne, Eddie Van Halen, L.L. Cool J., Bon Jovi, and Michael Jackson. Jackson's album *Thriller*, which sold 50 million copies is full of the occult. And there are many, many more.

Rock isn't the only offending style of music. Country and Western is far from being as pure as the driven snow. Some examples of that include songs like "It's All Wrong, But It's Alright," "When the Fire Gets Hot," "It's a Cheating Situation," and "To All the Girls I've Loved Before." Country singer and superstar, Dolly Parton, played the leading role in the movie, "Best Little Whorehouse in Texas." The "Big Band" groups aren't exactly spotless either. Many of the leading names produce music that promotes adultery and sexual relationships apart from marriage.

Straight Answers for Tough Questions
So what are we to do—float through life, humming hymns from the middle ages? Should we sell our stereos, CDs, tape players, and radios, vowing never to listen to music again? Do we throw out all rock and roll because of artists like these?

That's not necessary. The Lord gives straight answers to straight questions. Let's look in His book and learn how to sort this out. First Corinthians 10:21 says, "You cannot drink the cup of the Lord and the cup of demons too; you cannot have a part in both the Lord's table and the table of demons." In other words, we have to choose who is going to influence us. No one else makes that decision for us. Either we choose the Lord's way, or we don't.

If we follow the Lord's way, we have to examine *all* music with the light of Scripture. In other words, it would be helpful to learn to evaluate music using the four categories I suggested:

1. The music may be great, but the message isn't worth the powder to blow it off the page.
2. The message is good, but the music is awful.
3. Both the music and the message are great.
4. Both stink!

If the message in a song conflicts with the standards of the Word, we should junk it. Don't permit anything to enter your system that hinders your relationship with the Lord.

> I will set before my eyes no vile thing. The deeds of faithless men I hate; they will not cling to me.
>
> Psalm 101:3

For though we live in the world, we do not wage war as the world does. The weapons we fight with are not the weapons of the world. On the contrary, they have divine power to demolish strongholds. We demolish arguments and every pretension that sets itself up against the knowledge of God, and we take captive every thought to make it obedient to Christ. And we will be ready to punish every act of disobedience, once your obedience is complete.

2 Corinthians 10:3-6

Should you help the wicked and love those who hate the Lord?

2 Chronicles 19:2b

On the other hand, if the music does not conflict with the teachings of Scripture, and if a piece of music enhances your life, and you can enjoy it and learn to appreciate the quality and expertise required to produce it, then go for it!

Perhaps these questions will help you further in establishing a value system for music:

1. What are the people saying? What do they want me to do?

2. What is the lifestyle of the musicians? Should I support the attitude they promote?

3. Do those performing the music want me to be hindered in my walk with Christ?

4. If Jesus were to walk into my room, pull up a chair, and turn on my music, would I be embarrassed?

While I was sharing this at a youth camp in Pennsylvania, the Lord began to speak to different ones about their music. Nearly 50 teens came forward to repent at the end of the talk. After the service, Nicole and Jeanna asked if we could talk privately. They had gone back to their dorm, gotten some tapes the Lord had convicted them about, and asked if I would destroy them. I said, "No, I want you to have that sense of release." We agreed to smash the tapes and throw them into the dumpster. By the time we had made our way to the trash bin, about 12 others had made the same decision. Crushing the tapes on rocks and throwing them into the dumpster brought such a freedom, many wept with a new sense of joy. It was the highlight of the week.

This summer, while ministering at a camp in Georgia, a girl walked up to me, asking if I remembered her. Before I could recall exactly who she was, she said, "I am Nicole from Pennsylvania, and I trashed all my bad music last year at camp." Then she said, "And guess what? The amount of time I used to spend listening to junky music, I now spend studying. I am making straight A's. And you know what else? I have also memorized the Book of Acts word for word! My relationship with the Lord has never been better since I learned to evaluate music God's way!"

Alternatives to the Assaults

Learning to accept the idea that some music should take a roll because it assaults our relationship with God is difficult. But as believers in Christ, we should be cut by sinful ideas and direct insults to our Lord and what we believe. Fortunately, the Lord has raised up many godly groups that have phenomenal abilities in music. They combine both a message and music style that effectively communicate God's way. Some examples are Steve Camp, Steve Green, Truth, Sandi Patti, Wayne Watson, Dallas Holms, Ray Boltz, First Call, Michael W. Smith, Amy Grant, the Wynans, Twila Paris, The Brooklyn Tabernacle Choir, Hosanna! Music, Praise, Take Six, and dozens of others.

Hopefully this chapter has helped you sift through the issue of music, letting you know that the music style isn't the issue as much as the message being communicated. One thing is for certain—music affects us and can be a tool that can *in*crease or *de*crease our growth in Christ. Don't let the decline take place!

Calling It Straight

1. How important is music to you?

2. What albums, CDs, or cassettes did you buy this last year?

3. How do they measure up if you use the questions for establishing a value system on music?

4. Think about the music you listened to today. How does it meet the standards found in the Scriptures mentioned in this chapter? What should you do?

5. ABORTION: WAR ON THE PREBORN

January 16, 1991 is a day Americans should remember well. At approximately 7:00 P.M., the United States declared war on Iraq. Fighter planes struck Iraqi targets after Iraq ignored repeated warnings to remove troops from Kuwait. Live reports, aired on CNN and other networks, gave details of damages and the number of pilots missing. The American people wept as United States military personnel captured by Iraqi troops were forced to speak against the war and America while being "interviewed" on Iraqi television. Thankfully, the conflict was short-lived, despite the Iraqi scud missiles, the burning of oil fields in Kuwait, and loss of some American lives.

Today our country is engaged in another battle. Like the war with Iraq, this conflict began on a January day, but in 1973. The battle has become fierce, with the brutality at an unprecedented level. The losses in the campaign are staggering in comparison to any other in our nation's history. While Americans feared the illegal use of "mustard gas" while fighting against Iraq, the weapons in this fight have no legal limitations. With a calculated strategy, land mines have been planted underneath our value structure, sending shrapnel into our moral foundations. Some of the leading generals of America's Arch-Enemy come from the highest educational institutions in our land, while financial support for this war comes from the elite of society.

Who or what is causing this hostility, deeply wounding nearly every family in America? Who is undermining our values? Who is this enemy? It is none other than legalized abortion.

Basically there are three positions regarding abortion:

1. A woman has the right to choose to have an abortion, and the courts should make no legal reversals regarding this.

2. Abortion should only be allowed in cases of incest or rape.

3. Abortion is morally wrong and should never be allowed in any case.

What Does God Say?

It is good to know that Scripture gives answers to such heated issues. In the Bible we discover a direct answer from God about what is right and wrong. Here are some examples of what God says about men and women and their children.

> You shall not murder.
>
> Exodus 20:13

> If men who are fighting hit a pregnant woman and she gives birth prematurely but there is no serious injury, the offender must be fined whatever the woman's husband demands and the court allows. But if there is serious injury, you are to take life for life, eye for eye, tooth for tooth, hand for hand, foot for foot, burn for burn, wound for wound, bruise for bruise.
>
> Exodus 21:22-25

Here God says that killing the innocent is wrong. Additional proof of this is found in Deuteronomy 27:25:

> Cursed is the man who accepts a bribe to kill an innocent person.

Is there anyone more innocent than a preborn child?

The Bible also says this about the preborn in these passages:

> Before I formed you in the womb I knew you, before you were born I set you apart.
>
> Jeremiah 1:5a

> Yet you brought me out of the womb; You made me trust in You even at my mother's breast. From birth I was cast upon You; from my mother's womb You have been my God.
>
> Psalm 22:9-10

> For You created my inmost being; You knit me together in my mother's womb. I praise You because I am fearfully and wonderfully made; Your works are wonderful, I know that full well.

My frame was not hidden from You when I was made in the secret place. When I was woven together in the depths of the earth, Your eyes saw my unformed body. All the days ordained for me were written in Your book before one of them came to be.

Psalm 139:13-16

God designed a woman's body to protect and nurture her unborn child. He even knows a child's name *before* conception. Wow!

A Baby Lives Before It Is Born
These functions take place before the baby's birth:
- A heartbeat begins between the 18th and 25th day following conception.
- The foundation for the entire nervous system is laid down by the 20th day.
- At 42 days the skeleton is complete, and reflexes are present.
- Electrical brainwaves have been recorded as early as 43 days.
- The brain and all body systems are present by 8 weeks.
- If you tickle the baby's nose at 8 weeks, it will flex his head away from stimuli.
- At 9 to 10 weeks the baby squints, swallows, moves his/her tongue, and can make a fist.
- At 11 to 12 weeks the baby sucks his/her thumb vigorously and breathes amniotic fluid.
- Fingernails are present by 11 to 12 weeks, eyelashes by 16 weeks.
- All body systems are functioning by 12 weeks.

The "Brephos"
In the following passages, the Bible mentions chil-

dren or babies. The word used in each instance is *brephos,* meaning "breathing, nursing infant."

> People were bringing little children to Jesus to have Him touch them, but the disciples rebuked them. When Jesus saw this, He was indignant. He said to them, "Let the little children come to me, and do not hinder them, for the kingdom of God belongs to such as these."
> Mark 10:13-14

> ... from infancy you have known the holy Scriptures, which are able to make you wise for salvation through faith in Christ Jesus.
> 2 Timothy 3:15

Remarkably, Dr. Luke uses the same word, *brephos,* in Luke 1:41-44 in speaking of the baby yet inside Elizabeth.

> When Elizabeth heard Mary's greeting *the baby leaped in her womb,* and Elizabeth was filled with the Holy Spirit. In a loud voice, she exclaimed: "Blessed are you among women, and blessed is the child you will bear! But why am I so favored, that the mother of my Lord should come to me? As soon as the sound of your greeting reached my ears, the *baby* in my womb leaped for joy."
> Luke 1:41-44 (emphasis mine)

Obviously, God recognizes that a baby inside the womb is as uniquely human as a child outside the womb. Both are equally His special image-bearers. Psalms 127 and 128 also value children.

> Sons are a heritage from the Lord, children a reward from Him. Like arrows in the hands of a warrior are sons born in one's youth. Blessed is the man whose quiver is full of them. They will not be put to shame when they contend with their enemies in the gate.
>
> Psalm 127:3-5a

> Blessed are all who fear the Lord, who walk in His ways. You will eat the fruit of your labor; blessings and prosperity will be yours. Your wife will be like a fruitful vine within your house; your sons will be like olive shoots around your table.
>
> Psalm 128:1-3

However, not everyone shares the Bible's view of the preborn child. Some people think a woman's rights are more important than the life of her child. While not every question about abortion can be answered here, this chapter would not be complete without addressing several issues. I believe the majority of issues can be satisfied with the following. Fighting abortion is a battle, and the best way to win a conflict is to think through and know the strategy of the enemy.

Here Is Ammunition for the Battle

1. Doesn't a woman have a right to an abortion? After all, it's her body, and she should be able to make that choice and maintain her rights.

Response: Unfortunately, because society accepts this kind of thinking, 97% of abortions are performed for the sake of convenience. A pregnancy, many believe, interrupts school, a career, or even a care-free life. While many argue that a woman has a right to abort, another question arises from that thinking, "What about the rights of the unborn? Doesn't the child get an equal voice?" Not if he or she is aborted!

2. What if a pregnancy occurs in an unstable, unhealthy family? Wouldn't abortion be a better alternative than to burden an already weak home?

Response: Think about the following situation:

> A college professor of law loved to pose the same question to his first-year classes. Year after year he would peer over his glasses and study the faces of those sophisticated modern-thinking students. With a wily grin he always began... 'What would you recommend?"
>
> Every eye was on him. Nobody moved as he continued...
>
> "A certain man was rather ill-tempered— some might say occasionally brutal. According to a few reports he was a problem drinker, a weak leader in the home, and unable to hold a steady job. His wife was not well... fact is, she eventually died of the disease that had plagued her for years, tuberculosis. Of the seven children ultimately born to her, only three lived to adulthood.
>
> "At this particular time and in that region of the world the death rate among children was tragically high, three out of five. Plagues were not uncommon; typhoid fever, diphtheria, smallpox, and a half-dozen other treacherous diseases—including syphilis—were on the rampage.
>
> "After losing her first son less than two years earlier, when he was only six days old, the ailing, depressed woman discovers, much to her chagrin, that she is pregnant again."

The professor paused, glanced about the room, and returned to his original question. "Alright . . . what would you recommend?"

Logic took charge. Quickly the students thought through the threatening domestic situation, mentally computed the odds against the possibility of survival, and came to the same conclusion as all the other classes in years gone by. Unhesitantly, the great majority agreed: "Without question, abortion."

"Well, students," the professor replied. "you have just killed Beethoven."[1]

When people play God, disasters happen.

3. What if a woman is raped or incest takes place, causing her to become pregnant?

Response: While brutality of this nature is always an offense of the deepest magnitude, there are questions that must be considered regarding abortion:

   a. Should the sin of rape and incest be coupled with the sin of taking the life of the child conceived from the brutality? Not according to Scripture. A fetus is as human as a child already born.

   b. Should the baby be forced to pay the ultimate penalty of death for the misdeeds of his or her father? That is like saying an eight year old has to go to the electric chair because his or her father killed someone. What kind of justice is that?

4. What if the mother's health is in danger?

Response: Dr. C. Everett Koop, former Surgeon General of the United States, said that during his nearly 40 years of practicing medicine: "Never once did a case come across my practice where abortion was necessary to save a mother's life."[2]

5. What if someone has had an abortion or helped pay for it? Can they be forgiven?
Response: No matter what sin has been committed, the Lord can set people free! Here is the proof:

> If we confess our sins, He is faithful and just and will forgive us our sins, and purify us from all unrighteousness.
>
> 1 John 1:9

> Forget the former things; do not dwell on the past. See, I am doing a new thing! Now it springs up; do you not perceive it? I am making a way in the desert and streams in the wasteland.
>
> Isaiah 43:18-19

> Therefore, there is now no condemnation for those who are in Christ Jesus.
>
> Romans 8:1

Though abortion causes deep guilt, God's forgiveness runs deeper. What a joy to know God still receives sinners and pardons their poor choices if they are willing to repent.

6. What if I or someone I know is pregnant and does not want the baby? What should happen next?
Response: Contact a Christian crisis pregnancy center and get help. While an unwanted pregnancy can be embarrassing, DON'T ABORT! Many have regretted the decision to abort afterward. On the other hand, I have talked with many who did not abort. Though the pregnancy was unwanted or unplanned, they carried their babies full term. To this day, I have never met even *one* who regretted giving life to her baby rather than taking it.

7. What can I do to take a stand against abortion?
Response:
   a. Support Pro-Life groups. Nearly every community has one. Focus on the Family, with Dr. James Dobson, has other available resources. Call them at 1-800-A Family.
   b. Pray. Apply the power of prayer to abortion, the enemy of America.
   c. Be open to housing a mother. Thousands consider abortion every year, and one thing that can keep that tragedy from happening is the love expressed by the provision of a home. Dare to take that challenge.

Sanctity of Life
To emphasize the magnitude of the number of casualties in this war, I want to close this chapter with the following chart:

AMERICAN WAR CASUALTIES
Each cross-mark represents 25,000 people killed. The war casualties represent all American combat-related deaths.

War	Casualties	
Revolutionary War	25,324	†
Civil War	498,332	††††††††††††††††††††
World War I	116,708	††††
World War II	407,316	††††††††††††††††
Korean War	54,246	††
Vietnam War	58,655	††

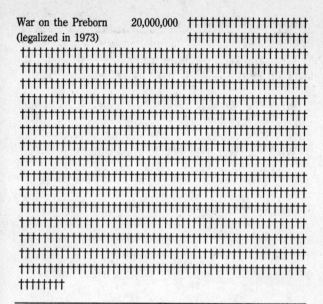

Unfortunately, this chart is inaccurate, for it only represents the years from 1973–1989. Every day in America, 4,400 babies are aborted.

Do you see why you are needed today in this conflict? God has spoken regarding abortion. What will be your response? I hope you will join His army. The preborn, the ones who can't fight for themselves, depend on you for their defense.

Calling It Straight

1. What are some common arguments heard today in favor of abortion? What is your response to each?

2. What does *brephos* mean? How do Mark 10:14 and Luke 1:40 fit together?

3. What can you do about abortion now?

6. GETTING A GRIP ON GUILT

*I*n my teen years and early twenties, I drove a 4 x 4 Jeep. It had mud tires, bucket seats, a roll bar, and airshocks to jack it up. I loved to go "mudd'n" and "four-wheel'n" in that Jeep. It became my identity. All my friends knew me by it. That Jeep was my "machine."

One day I noticed a red light flickering on the dashboard. After looking closer, I discovered the flashing light was indicating the oil was low. I had to make one of several choices:

   a. Act like I didn't see the light.
b. Take a crow bar, smash the dashboard, and say, "That's that."
c. Convince myself the Jeep had faulty wiring, and the signal really didn't mean anything.

d. Check the oil, add some if needed, and preserve the engine.

Fortunately, I chose the last option. Any other choice would have caused the engine to burn up, leaving me walking down the road talking to myself about the difference between the price of a quart of oil and a new engine.

In life, warning signals caution us. If we see spots, we know something is physically wrong. A caution light at an intersection means to be careful. A six-week failing notice sends a signal that we need to prepare our parents for what's coming on the report card. (ha!) However, another signal that blinks and requires our attention is called guilt. Our conscience uses our guilt to flash a message demanding attention immediately.

No one likes to be guilty, and most people will do anything to avoid it. It means we have made unwise choices.

In "The Tell-Tale Heart," Edgar Allan Poe writes about a killer who disposed of his victim's body under the floor boards of his house. Shortly afterward, a policeman arrived at the home to interrogate the man. Believing calmness could camouflage his guilt, the murderer placed a chair directly over the dead body under the floor as the policeman asked questions. As the conversation went on, the murderer began to hear a faint pounding in his head, like that of a heartbeat. His guilt began to show:

> No doubt I now grew very pale; but I talked more fluently, and with a heightened voice. Yet the sound increased—and what could I do? ...
> I talked more quickly—more vehemently; but the noise steadily increased. I arose and argued about trifles, in high key and with violent ges-

ticulation, but the noise steadily increased. Why would they not be gone?.. Oh God! What could I do? I foamed—I raved—I swore! I swung the chair upon which I had been sitting, and grated it upon the boards, but the noise arose over and continually increased... Was it possible they heard not?

"Villains!" I shrieked, "dissemble no more! I admit the deed!—tear up the planks!—here, here!—it is the beating of his hideous heart!"[1]

Different people react to guilt in different ways. In Irian Jaya, when people feel guilty for some wrong, they will cut off a finger of a young girl, hoping the evil spirits will be appeased by that sacrifice. Here in the U.S. when Susan slept with her boyfriend for the first time, she couldn't eat for a week from the guilt she felt. Steve found himself withdrawing from his family when his dad caught him smoking pot. Teresa responded to guilt just the opposite way. She began to do *extra* work around the house, hoping to get relief from the guilt she felt after cheating on a history exam. Tom, however, believed that no matter what he did, relief from guilt was hopeless. He had helped a friend break into the school and steal some records.

No matter how you react to guilt—with meanness, sleeplessness, aloofness, busy-ness or hopelessness, we all experience it. No one is exempt. When the guilt comes, it signals condemnation.

- You should be ashamed!
- This time, you've gone too far.
- Do you *really* think God will forgive you, again?
- Pack it in, pal! You're finished!
- Let's see, does this make 9,000 or 10,000 failures in this area?

- Are you back, AGAIN?
- What are you, retarded? Didn't you learn your lesson last time?

Getting a Grip
Because guilt is so universal and so forceful, we have to get a grip on it. To do that, let's focus on how guilt can be categorized and see how the Bible addresses this universal problem.

True or False
Guilt can be placed in one of two categories: true or false. True guilt occurs when we are genuinely wrong. Like the killer in the "Tell-Tale Heart," we can't hide it. False guilt, on the other hand, means we *feel* guilty; yet in reality, we are not.

A Closer Look
Most often false guilt comes because we convict ourselves and demand that we "pay." False guilt plays with our minds. We say things like, "I ought to do more," or "I should really be a better person," or even "maybe if I reach a higher level, I will impress God enough and He'll let me off the hook." False guilt is brutal because we are never sure we've paid the price.

Recently I heard about a mother who was walking with her daughter, and the little girl ran ahead to the street corner. Standing on the curb, she turned and asked her mother something. The mother didn't hear the question, due to the traffic, so she smiled and waved. The daughter smiled, waved back, and stepped into the path of a semi-tractor trailer, which killed her instantly. Apparently, she had asked her mother if she could cross the street and when the mother smiled and waved, the daughter thought her mother was saying it was OK. To this day, that mother believes she is guilty for her daughter's death. The false guilt is nearly choking her. She wonders what she did that was so awful that it caused God to allow her daughter's death.

Sometimes false guilt is inflicted on us by others. I heard about a lady who, at age 45, wrestles with the guilt of causing her house to burn to the ground when she was a little girl. The story goes that when she was 11 months old, she wouldn't stop crying, so, her parents said, God struck the house with lightning, totally destroying it with fire. Because this was pounded into her thinking since childhood, she feels totally responsible.

False guilt attacks every age group, Often I hear teens say they believe they are to blame for their parents' divorce. Comments like "If only I would have been a better kid," or "My grades should have been better," or "It's my fault" reveal the pain of false guilt that nearly crushes them.

Another form of false guilt can result from molestation or sexual abuse. Nothing affects people so harshly as this. Several dozen people have spoken with me about their horrible experiences. Without exception, every one of them believes they were to blame. Nothing could be further from the truth, but the false guilt has these people convinced they are at fault.

True Guilt

True guilt differs from false guilt. True guilt results when God's law is violated. The reason is simple; the Holy Spirit convicts us of sin. He doesn't make us go through a guessing game as to what we did wrong. He nails it specifically, as He did with David:

> When I kept silent, my bones wasted away

through my groaning all day long. For day and
night Your hand was heavy upon me; my
strength was sapped as in the heat of summer.
Then I acknowledged my sin to You and did not
cover up my iniquity. I said, "I will confess my
transgressions to the Lord"—and You forgave
the guilt of my sin.

Psalm 32:3-5

Because of Your wrath there is no health in my
body; my bones have no soundness because of
my sin. My guilt has overwhelmed me like a
burden too heavy to bear. My wounds fester
and are loathsome because of my sinful folly.

Psalm 38:3-5

The guilt David felt was a signal sent from heaven.
He chose to respond to the signal and was restored.

I will instruct you and teach you in the way you
should go; I will counsel you and watch over
you. Do not be like the horse or the mule,
which have no understanding but must be controlled
by bit and bridle or they will not come to
you. Many are the woes of the wicked, but the
Lord's unfailing love surrounds the man who
trusts in Him.

Psalm 32:8-10

Marie had been a prostitute and knew first-hand
what guilt felt like. After repeated abortions, she was
sure God would never forgive her. Though the signal
of heaven blinked constantly, she couldn't believe her
guilt could ever be relieved. But when she heard how
Christ could offer her hope, she experienced the joy
promised in God's Word.

> Praise the Lord, O my soul; all my inmost being, praise His holy name. Praise the Lord, O my soul, and forget not all His benefits—who forgives all your sins and heals all your diseases, who redeems your life from the pit and crowns you with love and compassion, who satisfies your desires with good things so that your youth is renewed like the eagle's.
>
> Psalm 103:1-5

> Yet to all who received Him, to those who believed in His name, He gave the right to become children of God....
>
> John 1:12

> Let us go right in, to God Himself, with true hearts fully trusting Him to receive us, because we have been sprinkled with Christ's blood to make us clean, and because our bodies have been washed with pure water.
>
> Hebrews 10:22 TLB

> Come, let's talk this over! says the Lord; no matter how deep the stain of your sins, I can take it out and make you as clean as freshly fallen snow....
>
> Isaiah 1:18 TLB

This message of hope so changed Marie she gladly accepted Jesus. Today, she often shares with others how her life is brand new.

God Can Make Guilt Disappear
As David and Marie found God's grace could remove their guilt, so you too can know that joy. Here is how.
  1. Learn to discern between true and false guilt.

True guilt matches up with Scripture. False guilt says things like, "You're so stupid!" "Even God won't forgive that!" "You are always so clumsy!" "All you are is wrong, wrong, wrong!" "It's all your fault!" We can inflict this on ourselves or have it thrown at us by others. Either way it is a choker.

2. When guilt is true, repent. The Holy Spirit confirms needed changes.

3. Trust Jesus with your guilt. All of us are guilty of sin by nature. We come equipped to violate God's holy laws (Romans 3:23). Often people think if they do enough good deeds they will balance out the wrong. However, the Scripture says: "For whoever keeps the whole law and yet stumbles at just one point is guilty of breaking all of it" (James 2:10). I once heard it explained like this: Suppose a person only sinned three times a day. That sounds nearly angelic, until we calculate it out.

$$\begin{array}{r} 365 \text{ days a year} \\ \times \quad 3 \text{ sins a day} \\ \hline 1{,}095 \text{ sins a year} \end{array}$$

Suppose a person lives 70 years.

$$\begin{array}{r} 1{,}095 \text{ sins a year} \\ \times \quad 70 \text{ years} \\ \hline 76{,}650 \text{ sins against God} \end{array}$$

Imagine standing in front of any judge with 76,650 offenses against the law. It would be curtains! Yet no matter how many offenses we commit against God, our guilt is met fully in Jesus.

Therefore, if anyone is in Christ, he is a new

Getting a Grip on Guilt

creation; the old has gone, the new has come!
... God made Him who had no sin to be sin for
us, so that in Him, we might become the righteousness of God.

2 Corinthians 5:17, 21

4. When Christ says you are free, receive it. When He frees us from sin, He throws a party!

In the same way, I tell you, there is rejoicing in
the presence of the angels of God over one sin-
ner who repents.

Luke 15:10

What are you guilty of? Can you tell the difference between false guilt and genuine guilt? Depend on the Holy Spirit to point out what is real and what isn't. Then depend on the forgiveness found in Christ. One thing is for certain: He will not send faulty signals to mislead you. Instead, He will keep you on the road to hope.

Calling It Straight

1. Define false guilt. Have you ever experienced it? How?

2. What is true guilt? Is there anyone who has never known true guilt? Why?

3. Are you experiencing true guilt about something? How can you get relief? Have you ever found this relief?

7. Anchors for Anger

While I was growing up in Florida, my family had a boat. I often spent weekends fishing the waters of South Florida. As a child, I remember discovering things like how the winch could pull the boat out of the water, how the running lights worked at night, and how the throttle controlled the speed. I also found out how the anchor could secure the boat in a storm. I also learned that if I held on to the anchor and fell overboard, I would sink to the bottom. I was impressed that such a small thing could control a boat, but I also recognized that it could bring harm if it were misused.

As an anchor can stabilize or bring harm, so anger can be a positive force in your life or a negative one. We all have the emotion of anger. We must learn how to let it work for us and not against us.

An ancient proverb says, "Whom the gods would destroy, they first make angry." That's true, for anger causes the heart to beat faster, blood pressure to climb, the eyes to dilate, the hands to get sweaty, the mouth to become as dry as cotton, the muscles to get tense and the adrenaline to flow. Every time we get angry, we activate all kinds of responses in our bodies.

Anger is as old as human nature. In Genesis, Cain was angry at his brother, Abel, so he killed him. In Luke, the elder brother of the prodigal son was angry because his father had a party when the younger son repented and came home. James and John wanted to call down fire from heaven because some people wouldn't listen to the Gospel. Peter, in the garden of Gethsemane when Jesus was arrested, picked up a sword and sliced off a guy's ear.

We all respond to anger in different ways. Thomas Jefferson said an angry person should count to 10. When he is very angry, he should count to 100. Mark Twain, 75 years later, said a person should count to four when angry, and when very angry, he should swear!

Growing up in an abusive home caused Angela to be angry. The prolonged illness that eventually took Eddie's father caused him to be nearly volcanic inside. Sara was born with a physical handicap, causing her to be treated "differently" by others. As a result, her "don't-get-near-me" angry attitude repels people.

Anger and Action
Research shows that anger can be categorized in five levels. The first is *mild irritation,* like when the class clown fires a spit ball at the back of your ear. The second level is *indignation.* That occurs when some-

thing unfair happens. Sam felt this toward his boss for not letting him switch shifts with another worker so he could attend the youth retreat. The third level of anger is *wrath*. When Kevin discovered someone had thrown a rock through his windshield, he was filled with wrath. The fourth stage of anger is *fury*. Fury can result in violence followed by temporary loss of control. As I am writing this chapter, the top story of the Atlanta news is about an eight-year-old in the ghetto who was killed as he was caught in a crossfire of bullets between a "crack" dealer and police. The fury in that section of town is clear. The final level of anger is *rage*. Rage results in violence done without knowledge. This level of anger is the ugliest. It causes people to murder and mutilate bodies without knowledge of what they are doing.

Misconceptions about Anger

Alex told me he couldn't control his anger. But when I asked him how he answered the phone when he was angry, he said, "Just like always." I responded, "Then you can control your anger, can't you?" He wasn't too happy to answer "yes," but he saw he had to.

Maggi believes she inherited her fits of anger from her Irish background. Therefore, when she is mad, she thinks everyone should live with it. Maggi may have inherited high blood pressure, red hair, fair skin, or even a lean body, but she didn't inherit anger. She learned it.

The Scriptures Speak about Anger, Pro and Con

Because anger can help us or kill us, we need to learn how to walk through this potential storm without getting blown off course. Smart people study the compass of the Scriptures to get answers to hard things in life. Let's do the same thing with anger and see when we should and shouldn't get angry.

Unjustified Anger

> But now you must rid yourselves of all such things as these: anger, rage, malice, slander, and filthy language from your lips.
> Colossians 3:8

> My dear brothers, take note of this: Everyone should be quick to listen, slow to speak, and slow to become angry, for man's anger does not bring about the righteous life that God desires.
> James 1:19-20

> Better a patient man than a warrior, a man who controls his temper than one who takes a city.
> Proverbs 16:32

> A man's wisdom gives him patience; it is to his glory to overlook an offense.
> Proverbs 19:11

> Do not make friends with a hot-tempered man, do not associate with one easily angered, or you may learn his ways and get yourself ensnared.
> Proverbs 22:24-25

The bottom line is this: unjustified anger will pull you under. A case in point is the situation in Texas where a girl was cut from the cheerleading squad. Her mother, Wanda Holloway, became so angry that she contracted a hit-man to kill the mother of another cheerleader, thinking the student would then drop off the squad due to grief. Then her daughter would be asked to fill in the slot. Fortunately, the news leaked out, and the plan was discovered. Mrs. Holloway was found guilty and sentenced to jail. Because she could not control her anger over her daughter not being selected for cheerleading, she will pay the price for the rest of her life.

Justified Anger

Electricity can be fatal, and fuel can be deadly to drink. However, if controlled properly, both are productive. Anger can be positive as well. Look at these verses:

> When Saul heard their words, the Spirit of God came upon him in power, and he burned with anger.
>
> 1 Samuel 11:6

> In your anger do not sin: Do not let the sun go down while you are still angry, and do not give the devil a foothold.
>
> Ephesians 4:26-27

What we find here is that it is OK to get angry, as long as the God-given emotion of anger is used legitimately.

Temper in the Temple

Jesus expressed His anger in many ways. When Jesus encountered those who knew the teaching of the coming Messiah but refused to believe He was the sent one, Jesus called them "blind fools." He called the Pharisees "white-washed tombs, full of dead men's bones," and "murderers" for they deceived people. But the ultimate example came when Jesus expressed His anger against the evil practices in the temple. The story goes like this:

> On reaching Jerusalem, Jesus entered the temple area and began driving out those who were buying and selling there. He overturned the tables of the money changers and the benches of those selling doves, and would not allow anyone to carry merchandise through the temple courts. And as He taught them, He said, "Is it not written: 'My house will be called a house of prayer for all nations'? But you have made it a 'den of robbers.'" The chief priests and the teachers of the law heard this and began looking for a way to kill Him, for they feared Him, because the whole crowd was amazed at His teaching.
>
> Mark 11:15-18

Jesus was angry at the evil and channeled His energies toward correcting the wrong. In this case, anger exercised against the wrong was right!

Recently I read about a bully in a school who thought he was "King of the Jungle." Then he met his match. Tony Campolo tells the rest of the story:

> In the somewhat violent high school subculture in which I spent my teenage years, there was a big tough guy who daily extorted money from younger students. It was not enough for him that he took money from boys who could never stand up to his bullying—but, at times, he would tell his victims to beg him to take their money. He got immense pleasure from forcing boys to do this in the presence of their girlfriends and then laughing at their humiliation.

One day at lunchtime, he picked on a boy whose brother was a 225-pound, six-feet five-inch center on the basketball team. Halfway through his extortion act, he felt a tap on his shoulder. He turned and was greeted by a solid punch to the stomach. In the face of the threat posed by his attacker, the tyrant became a sniveling coward begging not to be hit again. The crowd in the lunchroom roared with approval as the bully was told to get on his knees and beg for mercy. Not only did he do that, but he was forced to go to every other boy in the lunchroom and kiss his shoes. After that the bully transferred to another school. His public humiliation was more than he could bear. The rest of us were glad that he had gotten a taste of his own medicine. We felt he had had it coming.[1]

Mopping Up the Mess

To make sure you know how to handle anger, let's review what the Bible says. First, uncontrolled, unjustified anger is deadly. That is why the Bible says to stay away from angry people.

Second, controlled, justified anger is acceptable, but make sure you don't sin or give the devil a foothold.

Third, pick your battles. Do you want to know what is worth getting angry about? Try some of these:

- 1.5 million abortions happen in America annually, one half of them to teenage girls.

- 50% of all deaths on America's highways are because someone was drunk.

- One in three girls and one in five guys in America are forced into some sexual encounter with an adult before they are 18.

- Date rape happens every day.
- Pornography is an $8 billion business in the country that claims, "In God We Trust."
- The number one killer of teens in America is alcohol-related accidents.

These things are worth getting angry about because our anger comes from our compassion for the innocent, our love for the wrong-doers, and our desire to correct them. Learn to use anger for positive things as you allow the Holy Spirit to control you.

Calling It Straight

1. What are the five levels of anger? Which levels have you experienced? How?

2. Why is uncontrolled anger so deadly?

3. How would you have responded if you had seen Jesus throw the robbers out of the Temple?

4. What are you angry about? Why? What will you do or be if you don't control your anger? How can you channel your anger properly?

8. WHEN SELF-ESTEEM GROWS DIM

*L*ast year our family got a car that fit us perfectly. It was virtually brand new, with only 3600 miles. It looked sporty, got great mileage, and had a fairly decent stereo. There was only one problem. It had two headlights with minor cracks in them. Moisture had seeped in, causing metal inside the light to corrode. Instead of beaming a bright light, the headlights gave off a dull, yellowed ray. The reflection was so weak that I nearly drove into a ditch, ran over three neighbors, and hit our dog, all in one night! Until those headlights were replaced, driving at night was hazardous at best!

In many ways, we are like that vehicle. We motor along, performing well, getting from one place to another. However, due to a few "cracks" in our lives, we don't reflect the brightness we really have the capacity for. Sin has corroded our ability to shine as we were originally designed.

Dr. James Dobson tells about a man whose life had so many cracks that he was in total darkness. The results even blackened history:

> He began his life with all the classic handicaps and disadvantages. His mother was a powerfully built, dominating woman who found it difficult to love anyone. She had been married three times, and her second husband divorced her because she beat him up regularly. The father of the child I'm describing was her third husband; he died of a heart attack a few months before the child's birth. As a consequence, the mother had to work long hours from his earliest childhood.
>
> She gave him no affection, no love, no discipline, and no training during those early years. She even forbade him to call her at work. Other children had little to do with him, so he was alone most of the time. He was absolutely rejected from earliest childhood. He was ugly and poor and untrained and unlovable. When he was thirteen years old a school psychologist commented that he probably didn't even know the meaning of the word "love." During adolescence, the girls would have nothing to do with him and he fought with the boys.
>
> Despite a high IQ, he failed academically, and finally dropped out during his third year of high school. He thought he might find a new acceptance in the Marine Corps; they reportedly built men, and he wanted to be one. But his problems went with him. The other marines

laughed at him and ridiculed him. He fought back, resisted authority, and was court-martialed and thrown out of the marines with an undesirable discharge. So there he was—a young man in his early twenties—absolutely friendless and shipwrecked. He was small and scrawny in stature. He had an adolescent squeak in his voice. He was balding. He had no talent, no skill, no sense of worthiness. He didn't even have a driver's license.

Once again he thought he could run from his problems, so he went to live in a foreign country. But he was rejected there too. Nothing had changed. While there, he married a girl who herself had been an illegitimate child and brought her back to America with him. Soon, she began to develop the same contempt for him that everyone else displayed. She bore him two children, but he never enjoyed the status and respect that a father should have. His marriage continued to crumble. His wife demanded more and more things that he could not provide. Instead of being his ally against the bitter world, as he hoped, she became his most vicious opponent. She could outfight him, and she learned to bully him. On one occasion, she locked him in the bathroom as punishment. Finally, she forced him to leave.

He tried to make it on his own, but he was terribly lonely. After days of solitude, he went home and literally begged her to take him back. He surrendered all pride. He crawled. He accepted humiliation. He came on her terms. Despite his meager salary, he brought her seventy-eight dollars as a gift, asking her to take it and spend it any way she wished. But she laughed at him. She belittled his feeble attempts to supply the family's needs. She ridiculed his failure. She made fun of his sexual impotency in front of a friend who was there. At one point, he fell on his knees and wept bitterly, as the greater darkness of his private nightmare enveloped him.

Finally, in silence, he pleaded no more. No one wanted him. No one had ever wanted him. He was perhaps the most rejected man of our time. His ego lay shattered in a fragmented dust!

The next day, he was a strangely different man. He arose, went to the garage, and took down a rifle he had hidden there. He carried it with him to his newly acquired job at a book-storage building. And from a window on the sixth floor of that building, shortly after noon, November 22, 1963, he sent two shells crashing into the head of President John Fitzgerald Kennedy.

Lee Harvey Oswald, the rejected, unlovable failure, killed the man who, more than any other man on earth, embodied all the success, beauty, wealth, and family affection which he lacked. In firing that rifle, he utilized the one skill he had learned in his entire, miserable lifetime.[1]

If a person's self-esteem is abused enough, total blackness can take over, ruining not only that life but those around it as well. That is why a healthy, bright self-esteem is needed. This brightness doesn't come from just any resource, however. It has to come from the Designer of Lives, the Lord Himself. To find out how to have this bright light within us, we have to read the Owner's Manual, the Bible. But first, let's see what causes the dulling corrosion in our lives.

Too Big, Too Little
A quick look in the mirror for most people is like someone turning down a dimmer switch. Our self-esteem fades as we compare ourselves to others. We either think we are too big or too little. Here's what often happens:

Too Big	*Too Little*
nose	height
waistline	eyes
feet	legs
legs	arms
head	chest
ears	breasts
scars	coordination
pimples	muscles
family problems	friends

It doesn't take another Einstein to figure out that most of the time:
- The prettiest baby gets the most attention.
- The better athlete wins more scholarships.
- The more attractive people get the benefit of the doubt.
- The most popular become Homecoming Queen or King.
- The best personality becomes Student Body President.
- The best bodies get the dates and attention.

When we think these qualities are lacking in our lives, the light within begins to dim.

Repeated problems and hard times can also eat away at our self-esteem. Life's difficult experiences have a tendency to dull the brightness or eliminate it altogether.

Jack was sure the family was splitting up because he had argued with his parents about grades, music, dating, and clothes. When his mom and dad told him they were divorcing, it was like being in a cave without a lantern. Sharon can relate. While growing up, she was repeatedly molested by a friend of her family. When she became a teen, she attempted suicide three times. Each time she ended up in a mental hospital, which only increased her self-hatred. Denise went to a party one weekend, got drunk, and passed out. The next day she woke up in bed with someone she didn't know. To this day she is fearful of having AIDS and wonders what she will say to her future husband. Paul's future is dulled too. He was doing well in his classes, and scholarships seemed likely until he was caught cheating on a Calculus final. When the teacher caught him, it was like his future got on a jetliner and flew away.

Playing the Game: "Let's Fake 'Em Out"

When a person feels worthless, he or she also fears rejection, so he or she plays a game called, "Let's Fake 'Em Out." Here are some examples:

1. Mr. Defensive: This fake signal shouts, "I'm-in-charge-and-the-rest-of-you-jerks-stand-back." While someone may act like "Billy Bad," deep inside he feels terrible about himself.

2. The Funny Lady: The person who is always funny often hurts the most. Her laughter hides her hurt. Being the class clown is a great disguise, yet when the laughing stops, the silence is filled with pain. "Laughter cannot mask a heavy heart. When the laughter ends, the grief remains" (Proverbs 14:13, TLB).

Other Games

We use other ways to cover up the pain of low self-esteem. Randy, who feels he is too fat, doesn't respond to insults from classmates, yet deep inside the comments cut like razors. Cheryl plays the game of "I'll withdraw." She feels badly about her lanky frame, so she tries to be invisible. Annette does just the opposite. Her dad is an alcoholic and has made her feel worthless by his harsh words. To overcome this, she plays the game called "I'll conform." She will do anything to gain acceptance from others. Rich also plays a game: "Perfectionism." To him everything must be perfect, or he feels like a total failure.

Deliverance from "Dimness"

At times we all have poor self-images. I even heard Patrick Swayze say once in an interview that he is not really happy with himself. Remarkably, the interviewer said she struggled with her looks too. While it's hard to imagine "successful" people like this could be unhappy with their looks, we can understand the effects of a low self-esteem.

Scripture shows us the way out of the darkness of a poor self-image. Psalm 139 sheds some light for us:

> For You created my inmost being; You knit me together in my mother's womb. I praise You because I am fearfully and wonderfully made; Your works are wonderful, I know that full well. My frame was not hidden from You when I was made in the secret place. When I was woven together in the depths of the earth, Your eyes saw my unformed body. All the days ordained for me were written in Your book before one of them came to be.
>
> Psalm 139:13-16

Talk about a masterpiece! Our very persons are from the hand of God. Consider the inner workings of our bodies. David didn't understand DNA, proteins, enzymes, or even the cells in a human body as we do today. Yet science tells us that in every human cell there are 46 chromosomes. Contained within them is the activity of a city the size of Tokyo and the information equivalent to 4,000 library books!

Think about the heart—it beats 70 times a minute, 40 million times a year, and daily pumps seven tons of blood throughout the body, never stopping day or night!

The human eye is like a precision camera, equipped with depth perception. And a marvelously efficient windshield cleaning system operates every time we blink. Minolta, Cannon, and Nikon combined could never reproduce the abilities of the human eye—and God has given us two such wonders!

We have two ears which usher air waves into the eardrums, where the hammer and the stirrup (bones about the size of a letter on this page) transmit the air vibrations. Nerve endings or "strings" differing in length and tensions respond to the vibration rate, resulting in our hearing. The movement of the fluid within the tiny bones of the ear allows us to maintain our sense of equalibrium.

Holding all of this together is our skin. Within one square inch of skin, there are over 600 sweat glands, nearly 1,000 "signal senders," and more than three million cells. Part of the skin includes our fingerprints, each different from any others anywhere!

Our brains are a marvel to modern scientists. A brain has the capacity of working 24 hours a day for 75 years and never growing tired. The most advanced computer anywhere could never reproduce the workload or ability of our brains. To build such a computer would take a structure the size of the Empire State Building, yet God has arranged it to fit inside our skulls. Unbelievable!

There is even more to the human body—bones, muscles, lungs, and our ability to communicate. How does all of that occur? Because we *are* fearfully and wonderfully made by the Lord Himself, and because He made us, we are special!

Another way we can be assured of our self-worth is by looking at our relationship with the Lord. In Christ, we:

- Are more than conquerors (Romans 8:37).
- Escape the wrath of the judgment (1 Thessalonians 1:9-10).
- Are kings and priests (Revelation 1:6).
- Are the children of God (2 Corinthians 6:18).
- Have an advocate if we sin (1 John 2:1).
- Are annointed (1 John 2:20).
- Have power over fear (2 Timothy 1:7).
- Go directly to God in prayer (Hebrews 4:16).
- Have been set free (John 8:36).
- Have power over evil (1 John 4:4).
- Are no longer condemned (Romans 8:1-2)
- Are assured of Heaven (John 14:1-5).
- Are given a new life (2 Corinthians 5:17).

God's grace secures our reservation in Heaven where we will spend all eternity with Him. Imagine! God wants to be with us forever. Have you ever had relatives who came to visit and stayed too long? You wondered if they would *ever* leave. The Lord has made a way for us to live with Him forever, and He *never* wants us to leave!

Understanding this, we can't help seeing ourselves differently. This doesn't mean we are to get cocky or arrogant. Rather, we allow God's thinking to transform ours. God proved our value by sending Jesus to die for our sins, so we could have a relationship with Him again.

When John heard about his special relationship with God and his security in Christ, he no longer felt he had to conform to what others expected. Alice also lost the "herd mentality" when she discovered how God thought of her as His creation. She has decided to give her life to the One who gave His for her. John and Alice have found their identities and self-esteem in Christ. It is not always easy to maintain that, but they are working on the changes as they read passages like these:

> Let me say this, then, speaking for the Lord: Live no longer as the unsaved do, for they are blinded and confused. Their closed hearts are full of darkness; they are far away from the life of God because they have shut their minds against Him, and they cannot understand His ways. They don't care anymore about right and wrong and have given themselves over to impure ways. They stop at nothing, being by their evil minds and reckless lusts.
> Ephesians 4:17-19, TLB

> Do not conform any longer to the pattern of this world, but be transformed by the renewing of your mind. Then you will be able to test and approve what God's will is—His good, pleasing and perfect will.
> Romans 12:2

What You Are, What You Aren't

Discovering self-esteem in Christ is liberating. It allows you to be what you are and releases you from the frustration of trying to be what you are not.

That happens as your focus shifts from what the world says to what God says you are!

Dr. Charles Stanley offers this regarding our identity in Christ. Think through these questions:

1. Who created you?
2. Who chose you to live with Him forever?
3. Who holds the power of life in His hands?
4. Who is ultimately in control of all that goes on in the world today?
5. Who sent His Son to die for you?
6. Who promised He would never leave you?
7. Who promised to be available at any time?
8. Who has the power to bring about in your life all that He has promised?
9. Who has promised to structure your circumstances so that you will be brought to maturity?
10. Who has given you an eternal identity based upon His work?
11. With whom, then, does your true security rest?
12. What relationship is the true test of your significance?[2]

Personalizing this brightens your entire life, allowing your self-esteem to grow as you realize your identity is in Christ. Walk with the One who walked Calvary's hill for you and gave His life that your sins might be forgiven, and your identity will be secure for all eternity.

Calling It Straight

1. In your own words describe your self-esteem right now.

2. What is your self-esteem connected to? Will it last six months? Two years? Is it really worth it?

3. What do you think of your body? Are you satisfied with the creation God made in you?

4. Look up the passages listed about what is ours in Christ. What are you seeing differently about yourself after doing that?

5. Ask the Lord to help you focus on what you are and to release you from the frustration that comes with seeing what you aren't.

6. Take a long look in the mirror. Begin to work with what God has given you, and seek to improve that. Allow Him to teach you what is worthwhile and what hurts your self-esteem.

9. Dealing With My Doubts

I am glad I am a Christian. I have followed Christ since my teen years, and I have never been sorry. There are a number of reasons why I don't regret being a Christian, many of which I will share in this chapter. If you have never made the decision to accept Christ, perhaps after reading this chapter, you too will want to become a believer. If you have already made that great decision, hopefully, this will encourage you in your faith.

The Scriptures—True to Form!
First, I follow Christ because the Scriptures are accurate. God's Word is true, despite the efforts of many to disprove it. The predictions of the Bible are an example. In some instances, though written hundreds

of years before something occurred, the prediction came true exactly as the Bible said it would.

Imagine you are given the job of predicting which teams are going to play in the Super Bowl this year. Could you do it? Could you name the starting quarterback and the winning team, say who is going to score the most touchdowns of all the players, and predict what interceptions will be made? Could you do that?

Suppose you had to predict with 100% accuracy who was going to be playing in the Super Bowl in the year 2075. Could you do that? How about the year 2312? That would be impossible!

The Bible made many predictions, sometimes hundreds of years in advance. Deuteronomy 18:20 says about those who make predictions:

> "But a prophet who presumes to speak in My name anything I have not commanded him to say, or a prophet who speaks in the name of other gods, must be put to death." You may say to yourselves, "How can we know when a message has not been spoken by the Lord?" If what a prophet proclaims in the name of the Lord does not take place or come true, that is a message the Lord has not spoken. That prophet has spoken presumptuously. Do not be afraid of him.
>
> Deuteronomy 18:20-22

In those days a prophet had to be 100% accurate, so no one could mislead people in the name of the Lord.

The Bible predicted the coming of Christ over three hundred times. Let's look at eight of those three hundred predictions and consider their accuracy:

Micah 5:2 says:

> But you, Bethlehem Ephrathah, though you are small among the clans of Judah, out of you will come for me one who will be ruler over Israel, whose origins are from of old, from ancient times.

Micah made this prediction 400 years before the birth of Christ and was right on target when he said Jesus would be born in the city of Bethlehem.

Malachi 3:1 speaks of a messenger who would prepare the way for Jesus. History shows that messenger was John the Baptist.

Zechariah 9:9 predicts Christ would come into Jerusalem riding, not in a chariot, nor on a horse, but on a colt. This prediction came true on Palm Sunday, 400 years later.

Zechariah 11:12 tells us that the one who would betray Jesus would do it for 30 pieces of silver. Judas, one of Jesus' disciples, was that man.

Zechariah 11:13 predicts a potter's field would be bought with those 30 pieces of silver. This is exactly what happened with the money Judas returned to the Pharisees. They later buried Judas there after he committed suicide.

Seven hundred years before the birth of Christ Psalm 22 gives a picture of Christ's death.

Isaiah 7:14 predicted that Christ would be born of a virgin, a supernatural means of conception.

Isaiah 53:7, 9 speak of the trial of Christ and His burial in a rich man's tomb. That wealthy man was Joseph of Arimathea.

Grasping the Probability

To predict accurately even eight of three hundred

prophecies of Christ is significant. In fact, one professor did a study to figure out the probability of those prophecies coming true. After doing research, he discovered the answer to be equal to that of 1×10^{17} power.

To help us grasp the magnitude of that figure, consider this illustration:

> ... Supposing that we take 1×10^{17} silver dollars and lay them on the face of Texas. They will cover all of the state two feet deep. Now mark one of those silver dollars and stir the whole mass thoroughly, all over the state. Blindfold a man, and tell him that he can travel as far as he wishes, but he must pick up one silver dollar and say that this is the right one. What chance would he have of getting the right one? Just the same chance that the prophets would have had of writing these eight prophecies and having them all come true in any one man. ...[1]

This considers the fulfillment of only eight of three hundred prophecies. There are 282 left. Christ fulfilled every one of them! One reason I follow Christ is because the Scriptures are that reliable.

A Girl and a Miracle

Second, I am a believer because of the Virgin Birth. Luke 1:26-34 tells the familiar Christmas story. Mary was engaged to Joseph. As a young girl, 15-17 years old, she was probably all excited about getting married. Then one day she had a strange guest visit her:

> In the sixth month, God sent the angel Gabriel to Nazareth, a town in Galilee, to a virgin

pledged to be married to a man named Joseph, a descendant of David. The virgin's name was Mary. The angel went to her and said, "Greetings, you who are highly favored! The Lord is with you." Mary was greatly troubled at his words and wondered what kind of greeting this might be. But the angel said to her, "Do not be afraid, Mary, you have found favor with God. You will be with child and give birth to a son, and you are to give Him the name Jesus. He will be great and will be called the Son of the Most High. The Lord God will give Him the throne of His father David, and He will reign over the house of Jacob forever; His kingdom will never end." "How will this be," Mary asked the angel, "since I am a virgin?"

Luke 1:26-34

Without the Virgin Birth, the Scriptures aren't accurate, making Christ just another man. If He is just another man, He is a liar, meaning there is no redemption or forgiveness. If the miracle of the virgin birth is inaccurate, why believe any of the other miracles, including the resurrection?

Yet the Virgin Birth is true! Joseph didn't believe it either at first. He wanted to put Mary away, for he knew that if his fiancée was pregnant, he wasn't the father! But, as with Mary, an angel came and told him the truth. He then went through with the wedding plans, and he and Mary did not have sexual relations until after Jesus was born.

I am further convinced of the Virgin Birth when I consider the scene at the Crucifixion. The authorities condemned Jesus to die on the cross for claiming equality with God. (He affirmed the Virgin Birth by saying He was equal with God.) The Pharisees were

Dealing with My Doubts

there, along with some Roman guards, and a few others. John was also there, standing next to Mary, Jesus' mother. All she would have had to do to stop her Son's death is say, "Wait a minute! He is a lunatic. His claiming equality with God is not the truth. I can tell you exactly who His father is." That would have stopped the execution. But Mary never speaks. Why? Because she knew how He was conceived. I don't know a mother on earth who would not stop the death of her son if she could. Yet, Mary never spoke, for she knew the truth—Jesus was born of a virgin!

The Resurrection

Third, I accept the Christian faith because of the Resurrection. The Bible tells us that if the Resurrection isn't true, we of all men should be most pitied. Yet there was a resurrection. Here is some proof.

1. It changed the disciples. None of them believed the resurrection at first. Upon first hearing the Lord was alive, they denied the possibility. But after encountering the resurrected Christ, the disciples were changed. They saw and touched Him after His death. He even prepared breakfast for them beside the Sea of Galilee. They saw Christ speak to over 500 people at one time and witnessed His ascension into heaven. They were so convinced that all but one gave his life because of his belief. Peter, Andrew, Philip, James, Bartholomew, and Simon were all crucified because they would not deny the Resurrection. Matthew was killed with a sword. Thaddeus was shot through with arrows. James was stoned to death. Thomas died by the spear. John was exiled to an island as a prisoner because he believed. All these men went from hiding in an upper room like a pack of cub scouts to men of courage who believed the message of the Resurrection even to death.

2. Saul was another man changed by the Resurrection. At first he thought his assignment from God was to stamp out the church for preaching the Resurrection. His meeting the resurrected Christ drastically changed him. He was so changed he wrote half of the New Testament!

My faith is in Christ because I am satisfied with the defense of the Scriptures, the validity of the Virgin Birth, and the truth of the resurrected Chirst. This is the hope that changes people, for Christ changed me. I have followed Him from the time of my late teen years without regret.

If you have never received Christ, I challenge you to do that. The One of whom the Scriptures speak with accuracy was born of a virgin, came out of the grave, and cancelled sin! He has destroyed the powers of death and offers eternal life.

Calling It Straight

1. What do you believe to be true about the Scriptures? Are they just a collection of myths? Nice stories? Or are they really true?

2. Have you ever really thought about the Virgin Birth? Is it difficult for you to believe? Why?

3. In your opinion, why is the Resurrection so important? What if there had been no Resurrection?

4. After thinking through the things mentioned in this chapter about Christianity, what is your reaction? Is Christianity worthwhile? How does it compare to other religions? Has this chapter lifted some doubts or misunderstandings regarding Christianity for you? How?

10. PRAYER WITH A PUNCH!

*H*ave you ever heard a child pray? Often, it is tender, and without exception, it is always honest.

Here's what I mean:

Dear Lord,

Please take care of everybody in the whole world except the landlord.

I love you.

Gwen
age 8
Indianapolis[1]

Dear God,

Can you guess what is the biggest river of all of them? The Amazon.

You ought to be able to because you made it. Ha, ha.

Guess Who[2]

Once I heard about a kid who became a little confused while reciting the Lord's Prayer. "Our Father, which art in heaven," he began. "Harold be Thy Name."

While a child's prayer can be funny at times, prayer is anything but child's play.

Somehow, most of us do not equate prayer with excitement but rather with boredom or even snooze material. Often we associate prayer with some old lady praying for 20 minutes for Aunt Fanny who stubbed her toe and for Uncle Tom who stubbed his fanny. Who needs that?

Thankfully, powerful prayer does not require we "punch a clock," or kneel "x" number of hours before we get the Lord's attention. Don't get the idea, however, that the Lord is against long prayers. He enjoys that but doesn't "require" a certain length of time from you before He responds.

Promises in Prayer

Let's look at some of God's promises regarding prayer:

> Know that the Lord has set apart the godly for Himself; the Lord will hear when I call to Him.
> Psalm 4:3

> Then you will call upon Me and come and pray to Me, and I will listen to you.
> Jeremiah 29:12

> The Lord is near to all who call on Him, to all who call on Him in truth.
> Psalm 145:18

> Call to me and I will answer you and tell you great and unsearchable things you do not know.
> Jeremiah 33:3

> And I will do whatever you ask in My name, so that the Son may bring glory to the Father. You may ask Me for anything in My name, and I will do it.
> John 14:13-14

When we believe and act on these promises, our conversations with God will be more meaningful to us. Dan, a student, saw a difference in his prayer life when he realized the important role the Bible gives to prayer. Usually he prayed when he was in trouble or when asked to before meals. Now he prays more frequently and enjoys it, knowing the Lord enjoys his prayer time also. Patti also senses a punch to her prayer life since she saw how the Lord looks at prayer. Now she knows she isn't just speaking words into the air but is "connecting" with Christ Himself!

Being Heard in Heaven

While I was sharing this with a youth group in Florida, the young people asked questions like these:
- "Does prayer really make that much difference?"
- "What's it take to be heard in heaven?"

- "How can I become faithful in prayer?"
- "How can I fight against the devil through prayer?"

These questions prove teens are interested in prayer. Recent surveys, like the following reported in the Atlanta *Journal*, show that most teens share this interest and curiosity about prayer.

> Three out of four teenagers pray alone. And 44 percent of teenagers read the Bible in private—13 percent of them regularly.
>
> The report, based on a survey conducted by the Gallup Organization, with which the center is affiliated, says young women are more likely than young men to pray or read the Bible privately. Protestant teenagers are more likely to engage in those activities than Catholics, as are teenagers who live in the South and Midwest.
>
> About 83 percent of teenagers living in the South say they pray alone, and 55 percent say they read the Bible by themselves. Figures for prayer and Bible reading in other parts of the country are, respectively, 74 percent and 51 percent in the Midwest; 67 and 31 percent, East; and 68 and 45 percent, West.
>
> "The great majority of teenagers say they believe God loves them, and a surprisingly high number report they have experienced the presence of God," the report says.
>
> A large majority of teenagers, 86 percent, say they believe in the divinity of Jesus—that He is God, or the Son of God.
>
> The telephone survey of 513 teenagers 13 through 17 showed that 95 percent believe in God or a universal spirit and that 93 percent believe God loves them.[3]

Because we hunger for a meaningful prayer life and we believe God's promises about prayer, we need to know how to apply what God says to our lives. We need some practical help to personalize prayer.

Step 1: Get to Know God
Praying only when you are in a jam is like only talking to a friend when he or she can help you somehow. If someone did that to you, you would say he or she was just using you.

Getting to know God means spending time with Him. During those times with Him, learn to speak with Him. For some that means praying in words, while others sit quietly before Him, reading the Bible. Many people use a prayer journal, reviewing it over time to see what the Lord has done in their lives. No matter how you care to do it, get to know God. Your relationship with Him depends on it.

Step 2: Don't Be Afraid
For some, the idea of talking with God is like talking with the President—they don't know what to say. God knows our thoughts before we do, so we can speak with Him freely. Begin by praising Him for who He is and adoring Him for His love and grace. Acknowledge your sin, and thank Him for forgiving you. Realizing that God wasn't going to zap me in the head for my sins was the most liberating thing I learned in college. After that, I learned to enjoy the Lord without fear. You can too as you develop your relationship with Him.

Step 3: Schedule a Regular Time
Joshua 1:7-8 says this:

> Be strong and very courageous. Be careful to

obey all the law my servant Moses gave you; do not turn from it to the right or to the left, that you may be successful wherever you go. Do not let this Book of the Law depart from your mouth; meditate on it day and night, so that you may be careful to do everything written in it. Then you will be prosperous and successful.

According to the Scripture, we need a regular time for praying and meeting with the Lord. I know from experience that if I don't schedule an appointed time, I tend to miss my time with the Lord. A scheduled quiet time is like a date with someone. I would be rude if I said I would pick you up at 7:00 P.M. on Friday and then I showed up at 3:30 A.M. on Wednesday. Find a quiet time that works for you and guard it.

Step 4: Believe Big
I'm glad God is not limited by anything. As His people pray faithfully, remarkable things can happen. Here are some examples:

> And all things, whatever you ask in prayer, believing, you will receive.
> Matthew 21:22 NKJV

> If you abide in Me, and My words abide in you, you will ask what you desire, and it shall be done for you.
> John 15:7 NKJV

> Then you will call upon Me and go and pray to Me, and I will listen to you.
> Jeremiah 29:12 NKJV

Not even the ACLU can stop that kind of power.

One Tuesday night in late November, members of the Duncanville (Tex.) High School junior varsity girl's basketball team received rousing cheers from the home crowd—not just for their victory in the game, but for what they did after the athletic contest. Meeting at center court, joined by members of the other team, they knelt in prayer.

The cheers came because the girls had decided to pray despite a recent ACLU lawsuit over whether such center-court prayers could be allowed.

U.S. District Judge Robert Maloney of Dallas issued a preliminary injunction prohibiting school officials from organizing, encouraging, or participating in school prayer. But he also stated clearly that students were within their rights to pray voluntarily at school events—even on the court.

For more than 20 years, Duncanville basketball teams have prayed at center court, often accompanied by their coaches. Last spring a girl on the junior-high basketball team, with the aid of her father and the ACLU, challenged the practice. The Washington, D.C.-based Rutherford Institute defended the team.[4]

As you get to know God, learn to develop regular prayer habits, and learn to believe big, your prayer life will become mighty. It won't happen overnight any more than a person can lose 100 pounds overnight or bench press 300 pounds the first time. But you can improve with time.

Answers to Our Prayers
As you develop your prayer life, you will see that God

answers prayers in four different ways. Here is how I have personally seen that happen.

1. "I Thought You'd Never Ask!"

> Delight yourself in the Lord and He will give you the desires of your heart.
>
> Psalm 37:4

> You want something but don't get it. You kill and covet, but you cannot have what you want. You quarrel and fight. You do not have, because you do not ask God. When you ask, you do not receive, because you ask with wrong motives, that you may spend what you get on your pleasures.
>
> James 4:2-3

I remember a time when it seemed like I could not get what I wanted most. I was very discouraged about my writing. I had a burden to write to young men and women but couldn't find a publisher interested in my work. In fact, I had received over a dozen rejections on my first book. Feeling thoroughly disgusted, I held my manuscript over a trash can and said something like this, "Lord, please give me a publisher, because if You don't I am going to trash this stuff, and I will always question this burden I believed I received from You." It was as though God said, "I thought you would never ask, Les." I wasn't sure what publisher would respond, but I was sure God had heard me. Within a month an editor called and agreed to publish my first book, *Pulling Weeds*. What a joy to see how the Lord answered my heartfelt prayer.

2. "Yes, and There's More to Come!"

> Have I not commanded you? Be strong and courageous. Do not be terrified; do not be discouraged, for the Lord your God will be with you wherever you go.
>
> Joshua 1:9

While in college, I began sensing God was directing me into full-time ministry. I resisted fiercely, for I was petrified of speaking to a crowd. The thought nearly caused me to throw-up. During my first year after college, I began to think positively about the possibility of preaching. Until then, I was satisfied with teaching a Sunday School class or singing in the choir.

As the Lord began to speak clearly, I softened and said "OK, Lord, I'll be a pastor, provided You *promise* to go with me and give me courage." It was as if the Lord said, "Yes, and there's more to come." And did it ever come! Now I stand before nearly a thousand people five days a weeks in chapel services at the Christian college where I am the Campus Pastor. In the last five years, I have spoken at over 20 conferences and have the confidence that the Lord who said to Moses, "I will never leave you" is the same Lord who saved me and goes with me. *That* is an answer to prayer.

3. "When the Timing is Right."

A number of years ago, my brother-in-law, Steve, was very ill. Repeated surgeries failed to bring relief to his digestive problems, despite the confidence of some of the world's best surgeons and specialists at Duke University. Our family prayed, asking for a miracle. But each time the surgery was unsuccessful, and we felt confused about why God hadn't answered. However, Steve's wife, Kathy, believed the Lord was going to do a miracle when the timing was right. And did the Lord ever pull one off!

A conference of 150 doctors was being held at Duke University. Because of the uniqueness of Steve's problem, his physicians asked permission to perform another surgery on Steve as the group of specialists observed on closed-circuit television. Steve agreed, hoping for a success. The doctor, with the finest training in the world, was unable to accomplish what was needed. As the other 150 doctors were watching, however, suddenly Steve's system began functioning on its own. Though a very ill man until then, he immediately began responding, in spite of all of the unsuccessful medical treatment. Today we believe this was a direct answer to prayer, a miracle which came when the timing was right. In front of 150 doctors, God brought a man from death's door. Today, Steve is in perfect health.

4. "I Have Another Idea."

There are times when we pray one way, and God answers another. This isn't easy to accept, for most of us like to say, "OK God, here's the plan. Now, feel free to bless it." Occasionally, God has another plan. This is often hard to understand at the time, but as we walk with Him, we begin to see things as He does.

This was true for Ted and his wife. Jim, their son, was a great guy, who really was making a difference for Christ at his high school. He had led over 12 of his friends to the Lord. His parents had always prayed Jim would go into the ministry. But when the news came Jim had been killed in an accident, his parents were stunned. However, within six months after his death, nearly 50 people had committed themselves to serving the Lord in some full-time capacity. It was then Ted and his wife saw that God was saying, "I have another idea." It is this hope that keeps them from being bitter toward the Lord.

After reading this chapter, you can see prayer doesn't have to be "snooze material." It can be exciting. What a thrill to be part of God's program! Listen to this:

> Have you heard the story of Walter Vivian? He was an official of the Columbia Broadcasting Company. Columbia was to transmit King George's speech to the London Naval conference in 1930. The story is told about how moments before the broadcast, Vivian discovered a severed communication line. There was not enough time to repair it and still broadcast the king's message. So Vivian, committed to getting the broadcast through, grabbed a wire in each hand to restore the current. He was shocked and severely burned, but by standing in the gap, the message was heard throughout the land.
>
> King Jesus has a message that must be proclaimed! And every Christian is called to make sure that that message is heard. Men, women, teenagers, and children can all stand in the gap.[5]

As you dare to pray, results and answers will come. The power of God will be unleashed, boldness will be yours, anxiety will be replaced with peace and joy, and all this will be done for the glory of the Lord!

So buckle your seat belt—it's time to pray!

Calling It Straight

1. What have you believed about prayer before reading this chapter?

2. How is your thinking different now? What caused the change?

3. Review the four ways to pray and the four ways God answers prayer. How have you seen that personally?

4. Could you receive the challenge to begin to pray with power? Why?

5. Try meeting the Lord every day for a month. Do your best to be as faithful in your prayer time as you would be to a ball practice. Record the differences you observe in your life.

11. POWER! POWER! POWER!

When we think of power, many symbols come to mind. The "Power I" is a play in football. Cheerleaders do a cheer called "Power." Body builders do "power lifting." There is nuclear power, electrical power, horsepower, and word power. There are even "power clothes." It seems as though power is "in," and the days of kicking back and yawning through life are "out." To make a difference today requires power.

Thankfully, serving the Lord is not a boring, dusty, "ho-hum" life. Rather, it can be a life-changing, power-packed experience that comes when people dedicate themselves to Him. The believer's power comes from the Holy Spirit. Without Him, however, the Christian life is as powerless as a dead battery in a car at 30 below zero!

Terms that Confuse

Christians have different opinions about the Holy Spirit and the effects He has on a life totally surrendered to Him. Sometimes terms like "filled with the Holy Ghost," or "baptized in the Holy Spirit," or even "receiving the Second Blessing" are scary and cause people to shy away from the subject of the Holy Spirit. Yet the Scripture says God wants every believer to be filled with the Holy Spirit. Billy Graham said this, "I believe the greatest need is that men and women who profess the name of Jesus Christ be filled with the Spirit, and if you are not filled with the Spirit, you are sinning against God."[1]

A lot of people have questions about being Spirit-filled. Some people ask:

1. Does a Spirit-filled believer have to speak in tongues?
2. Isn't the believer filled at salvation?
3. Is this some kind of mystical experience?

What Does All of This Mean?

I believe people today want to have a life that is powerful and victorious, but they don't want to feel as though they are being tricked into a gimmick or fooled by an emotional ploy. We need a handle on these and other questions. So let's see what the Scripture says.

Tongues and Today

When we use the word "tongues" in the context of being Spirit-filled, we mean the ability to speak or pray in a language never studied or learned. Many charismatic churches say tongues is *the* sign or proof a person is filled with the Holy Spirit. The problem with this position is that if a person filled with the Holy Spirit must speak in tongues, then Billy Graham, Jonathan Edwards, the Wesley brothers, George Whitefield, D.L. Moody, Charles Stanley, Chuck Swindoll, Josh McDowell, Dr. James Dobson, Philip Yancey, Tony Campolo, and Chuck Colson all missed it! While tongues is a *viable* gift today, it is not *the* proof of the Spirit's presence in a person's life. Some of the most godly people and the most faithful prayer warriors I have ever met have never spoken in tongues. At the same time, I have met people with the gift of tongues who had a very powerful, solid relationship with the Lord. The bottom line regarding tongues and being Spirit-filled is that the Bible never proclaims the gift of tongues is *the* evidence of the Holy Spirit's presence, rather a life of holiness and power is the evidence, according to Galatians 5:22-23, "But the fruit of the Spirit is love, joy, peace, patience, kindness, goodness, faithfulness, gentleness, and self-control."

Wasn't I Filled At Salvation?

The Bible gives us some insight for this question:

> And you also were included in Christ when you heard the word of truth, the Gospel of your salvation. Having believed, you were marked in Him with a seal, the promised Holy Spirit . . .
> Ephesians 1:13

When we received Christ as Savior, the Holy Spirit was deposited in us. It is the same idea as money being deposited into an account so checks can be written against that account.

The depositing of the Holy Spirit in a believer can also be compared to an engagement ring. When I asked Kay to marry me, I went to the jewelry store and selected a set of rings. One was an engagement ring and the other was a wedding band. To prove my commitment to her, I gave her the engagement ring. On our wedding day, I gave her the wedding ring, sealing my pledge to stay true to her.

The same thing happened when we received Christ. The Spirit of God sealed us until the day of Jesus' return. What a day that is going to be! Until that day, as believers we are to be filled with the Holy Spirit, who gives us power. The Scriptures say:

> Therefore do not be foolish, but understand what the Lord's will is. Do not get drunk on wine, which leads to debauchery. Instead, be filled with the Spirit.
>
> Ephesians 5:17-18

I used to have questions about that verse. Why would liquor and the Lord be compared to each other? Then I discovered the answer. Liquor intoxicates, causing a loss of control; the Spirit invades, giving God total control. Being filled with the Spirit of God is a direct command. Did we receive the Holy Spirit at salvation? Absolutely! Yet the work of the Spirit is to be an ongoing process, a continual empowering by the Lord.

Is This to Be a "Mystical" Experience?

To some, the idea of being filled with the Holy Spirit seems risky. They either equate it with New Age teaching, don't know what to expect, or are leery of an "emotional experience," so they avoid it completely. I remember being skeptical myself. The last thing I wanted to be was some whacked out weirdo who walked around "high" on God. I settled the issue with this: I believe it is wrong to seek an emotional or mystical experience. We should not demand any gift, because the Scripture tells us that the Spirit gives gifts as He wills. Neither should we seek some kind of quick "spiritual fix." It is normal, however, to seek all of God and by faith to receive the fullness of God. It is the norm for the Christian to experience powerful, victorious living. God said that, and we should focus on this truth. Look at this:

> So I say to you: Ask and it will be given to you; seek and you will find; knock and the door will be opened to you. For everyone who asks receives; he who seeks finds; and to him who knocks, the door will be opened.
> Luke 11:9-10

> If you then, though you are evil, know how to give good gifts to your children, how much more will your Father in heaven give the Holy Spirit to those who ask Him!
> Luke 11:13

I have two children, Les Jr. and Philip. I enjoy many activities like teaching the Bible, writing books, talking to people, and traveling to speak at conferences. I do those things often and am grateful for the opportunity. But I also enjoy very much being a dad, especially at Christmas and on my kids' birthdays. Kay and I sneak gifts into the house, hide them, and anticipate the expressions on their faces when they open their presents. (In fact, while I write this chapter, we have worked out a plan to sneak a new bike from our home in north Georgia to south Florida where we will spend Christmas vacation with family.) We want the gift to be extra special. We enjoy showing them we are taking care and providing for them.

If our sons ask for something and we can provide

it, we gladly do so. It is a joy to meet their needs and, most of the time, even their wants. How much more will our Heavenly Father give the Holy Spirit to those who ask! However, receiving the Holy Spirit is not so we will have a new toy, but that we might have power! Acts 1 tells us:

> For John baptized with water, but in a few days you will be baptized with the Holy Spirit. . . . But you will receive power when the Holy Spirit comes on you; and you will be My witnesses in Jerusalem, and in all Judea and Samaria, and to the ends of the earth.
> Acts 1:5, 8

Acts 4:31 tells us that when the apostles had prayed, the place where they had gathered was shaken, and they were filled with the Holy Spirit and boldness! How? Because the Holy Spirit gave them power. According to the Scripture we are also to be filled continually in a new and fresh way. Thankfully, what God offers is not old, stale, or cold. He gives us something fresh.

My good friend, Fred Hartley, writes about the time he first experienced the Lord's power this way. For a while he was convinced that all he ever needed was given at salvation. Yet, he discovered he was empty and powerless. He wanted God to do something new for him. He writes about that experience of asking God to fill him with the Holy Spirit. This was a prayer he offered that day:

> Jesus, in no way am I ungrateful for your salvation because your death for me is the greatest expression of love I will ever know. I was an unworthy wretch when your grace reached out

to me. I know I am saved, but now I have a deep longing within my soul. I need to know that I have all of God without measure and I know you desire to fill me. So right now, fill me. Saturate me, every area of my life, every cell of my body, every thought. Immerse me in Thy Spirit. I receive this by faith, and I will never again doubt whether or not I have been filled. I know I am filled. Praise you in Jesus' name. Amen.[2]

It was a very simple prayer of faith. He then got up from his chair. No lightning bolt struck him behind the ear. No significant miracle happened. There was no particular change, yet there was a deep assurance that his prayer would be answered because he had prayed in faith.

Fred noticed that over the next two or three months six distinct changes came into his life.
- *Deep conviction of sin;*
- *Praise;*
- *Prayer;*
- *The fruit of the Spirit (Galatians 5:22-23);*
- *Gifts of the Spirit;*
- *Power in ministry.*[3]

From then on Fred was different. Two months later I met him. He so influenced my life that I haven't been the same since. Those personal changes came because Fred was Spirit-filled.

You might hear this and say, "Wow! I really want something like that! That is something I have longed for." Are you sure? Before you jump, think some things through:
- Do you want the Holy Spirit to be Lord over your life? Or do you want His benefits? (There is a big difference.)

- Do you really want to be possessed by the Spirit?
- Can He enter every closet of your life and have no key withheld?
- Can He have your value system?
- Can He have your prayer life?
- Can He have your personality, your future?
- Can He have your spending habits?
- Can He have your self-righteousness? Your agenda?
- Can He have your self-pity?
- Can He begin mighty things within you?
- Can He have your moodiness?
- Can He have your anger? Your evilness? Your bitterness?
- Can He blow out the dust of your heart and fill you with new enthusiasm?
- Can He come in power and convict sin in every area?
- Are you really willing to be obedient?

Can't you stay the way you are now? After all, you go to church, read the Bible, sing choruses, tithe occasionally, are honest, date nice people. Do you need something besides that? Do you want power, or do you want popularity? Are you hungry for God?

If you are, there is great news! God loves to fill people with Himself.

Being Filled with Power!

If you long to be filled with the Holy Spirit, according to the Scripture, this is what is to happen:

1. Romans 12:1-2 tells us to present our bodies as a living sacrifice.

2. Luke 11 tells us to ask our Heavenly Father for what we need.

3. We have to seek from Him the newness of life.

4. We have to agree with the Spirit and go in faith.

Is there a need in your life for that? If so, it is something you have to ask of God. No one can do it for you; not your elder, or your parents, or your girlfriend/boyfriend, Sunday School teacher, or Pastor. It is up to you and God.

Do you want to filled with the Holy Spirit? He comes that we might have power, joy, and a life of holiness. Seek Him for all His fullness, and allow God to fill your life with power, joy, and His Spirit.

Calling It Straight

1. What was your understanding of the Holy Spirit before reading this chapter?

2. What do you think now? Do you see a need to be filled with the Holy Spirit?

3. Look over that list of questions again and see if you really want to be filled with the Holy Spirit. What is your reaction to the total Lordship of Christ? Or do you just want to receive the benefits of being saved?

4. Review that list again on how to be filled with the Holy Spirit. If you have followed that, ask the Lord to confirm for you that you are now different.

12. GETTING DRESSED FOR THE DANCE

I didn't miss a dance all four years of high school. To me, the dances were the lifeblood of the school year. I would ask a girl at least two weeks early, buy my tickets, and begin to dream about how my date and I would look together. I saved my money for our dinner at the best restaurant in town. I even volunteered to wash and wax the family car so I could "arrive" in style. I often bought new clothes and made sure I looked sharp. I made sure the corsage matched my date's dress. It was fun looking and being at my best, and I enjoyed going first-class all the way.

Some guys are not like that. A guy might ask his date to the dance at 2:30 Friday afternoon, telling her he'll pick her up at 6:00. Then to top things off, he arrives at her house driving a backhoe, and takes her to eat at Burger King. The worst is he makes her pay, saying the cost of diesel fuel for his tractor has skyrocketed! He is kind enough, however, to stop and dig up some wild flowers along the road with the front-end loader, so she can have a corsage like the other girls.

Just as there are two ways to approach attending a dance, there are also two ways to approach dancing against the devil. You can either be prepared and ready and at your best spiritually or shuffle your way through your spiritual life.

Hopefully, this book has done more than condemn rebellion, immoral dating styles, junky music, and abortion. I don't want you to *feel* guilty. I want to show you how to handle guilt, as well as anger, low self-esteem and doubts about the Christian faith. Hopefully, you will experience a *great* prayer life because this book helped you. I want you to know the power of the Holy Spirit and not just the weakness of the flesh. I want you to experience a difference in your spiritual life and not be yanked around by the devil like a rag doll in a dog's mouth. I want you to feel more capable of handling the temptations of the devil, realizing you don't have to dance *with* him—you can dance *against* him, knowing that if you resist him, he *will* flee.

To do that, however, requires more than just some promises to "try to do better." According to Ephesians 6:10-18, we have to get dressed spiritually!

> Finally, be strong in the Lord and in His mighty power. Put on the full armor of God so that you can take your stand against the devil's schemes. For our struggle is not against flesh and blood, but against the rulers, against the authorities,

against the powers of this dark world and against the spiritual forces of evil in the heavenly realms. Therefore put on the full armor of God, so that when the day of evil comes, you may be able to stand your ground, and after you have done everything, to stand. Stand firm then, with the belt of truth buckled around your waist, with the breastplate of righteousness in place, and with your feet fitted with the readiness that comes from the Gospel of peace. In addition to all this, take up the shield of faith, with which you can extinguish all the flaming arrows of the evil one. Take the helmet of salvation and the sword of the Spirit, which is the Word of God. And pray in the Spirit on all occasions with all kinds of prayers and requests.

Ephesians 6:10-18

For a guy to neglect putting on *all* of this armor would be like wearing a tuxedo to a dance without shoes! Imagine this conversation:

PARENTS: Son, you look so good in your tux. It really fits great. But what about your shoes? You don't want to forget those.

SON: Naw. My feet always get so hot in those things. I'll just go barefooted. Besides, my date won't mind. She's a good dancer and won't step on my toes too many times.

Wouldn't that be wild? If a girl doesn't put on the full armor of God her outfit would be equally incomplete. Here's what I mean:

PARENTS: Sweetheart, you are such a beautiful

young lady. Any guy going to the dance with you will be envied. I can't wait to see you in your new dress.

DAUGHTER: Actually, Mom and Dad, I thought I'd just wear a pair of long pajamas tonight to the dance. I tell you, by the time we go out to eat, talk to people, get pictures taken and dance, I will be so tired, I could go right to sleep! My date won't mind too much. After all, he said to wear something comfortable that looks good on me. This should do the trick!

Wouldn't that be strange? It is equally strange not to be fully dressed against the works of the devil. With even one piece missing, we make it more difficult to dance our way to victory over him.

Armed with Armor
Since we need every piece of armor mentioned in the list recorded in Ephesians 6:10-18, let's look at each item individually and see the purpose of each one.

1. The Belt of Truth
Paul is talking here about a very important piece of equipment for a soldier. This belt was made of thick leather and looked similar to a nail-apron. It had hooks and pouches on it where the soldier would place his sword and support his shield. It also protected his abdominal area, yet was flexible enough to be used in battle or even hand-to-hand combat.

As the belt was essential to the soldier, the truth is essential in the believer's life. If we don't know what is true, we don't know what is false. The Bible says this about God's truth:

All Your words are true; all Your righteous laws are eternal.

Psalm 119:160

To the Jews who had believed Him, Jesus said, "If you hold to My teaching, you are really My disciples. Then you will know the truth, and the truth will set you free." ... So if the Son sets you free, you will be free indeed.

John 8:31-32, 36

Jesus answered, "I am the way and the truth and the life. No one comes to the Father except through Me."

John 14:6

Sanctify them by the truth; your word is truth.

John 17:17

Finally, brothers, whatever is true, whatever is noble, whatever is right, whatever is pure, whatever is lovely, whatever is admirable—if anything is excellent or praiseworthy—think about such things.

Philippians 4:8

While the Bible calls the devil the father of lies, Jesus is known as the truth. Therefore, when we decide to follow the Lord with all our hearts, God shows us the true meaning of life. As the soldier would hang his other equipment on his belt, so the believer hangs his faith on the truth in Jesus Christ!

2. The Breastplate of Righteousness
This piece of armor was often made of thick leather also, but the front was covered with a sheet of metal.

The breastplate covered the chest area, protecting the heart, lungs, stomach, and other vital organs. Should even one of those vital organs be hurt, the soldier was a "goner."

As the breastplate protected the man, so the righteousness of Christ protects our inner man. Without His righteousness, we would have no hope. The Bible says this:

> God made Him who had no sins to be sin for us, so that in Him we might become the righteousness of God.
>
> 2 Corinthians 5:21

> For in the Gospel a righteousness from God is revealed, a righteousness that is by faith from first to last, just as it is written: "The righteous will live by faith."
>
> Romans 1:17

> But now a righteousness from God, apart from law, has been made known, to which the Law and the Prophets testify. This righteousness from God comes through faith in Jesus Christ to all who believe. There is no difference, for all have sinned and fall short of the glory of God, and are justified freely by His grace through the redemption that came by Christ Jesus.
>
> Romans 3:21-24

The righteousness we have with God is because of our faith in Christ. Left to stand on our own against the devil, we would be knocked out cold instantly. But Christ has given us His pure righteousness in exchange for our impurity. As the soldier's breastplate protected his vital organs thoroughly, so

Christ's righteousness protects us completely.

3. Shoes for the Gospel of Peace

For shoes, the soldiers in New Testament days wore what we call sandals. They had hard leather soles, with straps that wrapped around the feet up to the shins. Often these shoes had nails in the bottom to help in climbing hills as well as for causing harm to enemies as the soldiers kicked or stomped them. Without good footing the soldier was unstable, and the instability caused insecurity and anxiety.

In combat against the devil, we too need sure footing. Our assurance comes from the peace of the Gospel of Christ. Before coming to Christ, we were enemies against God, but now we are friends with Him through the work of Christ. A name for Christ in Isaiah 9:6 is "Prince of Peace." Once there was a spiritual wall between us and God, but that wall is removed, and we are restored in our relationship with God through Christ.

That is what the Gospel of peace did for Larry. Bitter and angry at life, he tried drugs to escape. Nothing worked for him until the day someone introduced him to the Prince of Peace. Result: today he is raising his family to serve the Lord and realizes they too can find stability in Christ by exchanging insecurity and anxiety for peace.

4. The Shield of Faith

The shield was very important to a soldier. Made of leather and framed in metal, it resembled a door in size. Soaked in water, the shield was an excellent protection against fiery darts or arrows. Because the shield was so large, it easily protected a man completely.

Because of our faith in Christ, we too are protected

completely from the fiery darts of our enemy, the devil. Notice what the Scripture says about this essential piece of armor called "faith":

> Consequently, faith comes from hearing the message, and the message is heard through the Word of Christ.
>
> Romans 10:17

> Therefore since we have been justified through faith, we have peace with God through our Lord Jesus Christ.
>
> Romans 5:1

> We live by faith, not by sight.
>
> 2 Corinthians 5:7

Therefore, we combat the enemy by our faith in Christ. Our shield of faith protects us top to bottom against fear, insecurity, and uncertainty!

5. The Helmet of Salvation

The helmet was the most costly and ornate piece of armor the soldier wore. Covering the entire head, it protected the brain, which controls the entire person.

As the helmet covered the head, so salvation covers the entire person. At salvation, a person's sin is covered over, and a newness of life enters in. Salvation was costly, for Jesus paid sin's debt. Our salvation, therefore, should be the most obvious and attractive thing about our life.

6. The Sword of the Spirit

When we think of a sword, most of us think of a three foot long piece of sharpened metal hanging off the hip of a captain in the cavalry. This is not the type of sword talked about here. This sword was more of a dagger, used in hand-to-hand combat. If an enemy got past the other protection, the sword was a soldier's personal protection held up close to the body, for personal assurance.

The Bible is the sword for believers. It is to be tucked into our very beings, giving protection against the enemy. There are times when we wrestle against the devil. We dare not try to defeat him alone, but respond as Jesus did to him when being tempted. Read the story of Christ's temptation in Matthew 4 and you will see Jesus' repeated response, "It is written; ... It is written; ... " God's Word ought to be available to us, ready for us to use when the devil tries to tempt us.

This last Christmas I bought myself a new Bible. I am writing notes in it, underlining verses and making it mine. Before long, I will have read it cover to cover and as I read, it will be like a dagger in my hand against the devil.

A final note about the armor of the soldier. All of these weapons were for the front of the body. There was no protection for the back. In other words, a soldier had to advance. Retreating was not an option!

When you think about it, we don't have an option as to whether we will fight against the devil or not. As a believer, you are on the devil's "hit list." He wants to defeat you. We have a choice about how we will respond. We can be prepared and advancing, or we can be careless and sloppy.

The choice is yours. Dare to put on the *full* armor and advance!

Calling It Straight

1. Why bother to dress appropriately for a special occasion? What impression does that make?

2. In your own words, describe the connection between a soldier in the New Testament and a dancer against the devil.

3. Review the list of weapons again:
- Belt of Truth
- Shoes of the Gospel
- Helmet of Salvation
- Breastplate of Righteousness
- Shield of Faith
- Sword of the Spirit

Which are you most familiar with? Which needs your attention now?

4. What happens if a soldier runs from the battle? What happens if a believer doesn't want to dance against the devil in the power of the Spirit?

13. GOD IS STILL CALLING CHAMPIONS

One of the most exciting days I had in high school was the day Larry Czonka visited our campus. He was the fullback for the then World Champion Miami Dolphins. Czonka was so strong that he earned the nickname "Bull." A minimum of two defensive players were needed to tackle him. He was a key reason Miami gained (and still holds) the NFL record for the most games won consecutively. Shaking hands with a world champion like Czonka was the thrill of my life.

Because of his age, Czonka is no longer a world champion. In fact, the last time I saw him on TV, he wasn't scoring a touchdown; he was doing a beer commercial. What a waste! I remember thinking, "Czonka's championship was short-lived. I'm glad I serve the One who calls people to be champions forever."

The Need for Champions

We live in a day unlike any other in history. Families split apart like old denim jeans. Assaults in neighborhoods are at an all time high. There are 250,000 teenage prostitutes in America. Legalized abortion has taken the lives of millions of unborn babies since 1973. Gangs control our streets in many cities. AIDS threatens mankind everywhere. Integrity, once found in leaders across our land, has become nearly extinct. Where our schools once set standards for moral conduct, they now seem to encourage promiscuity by issuing condoms and advocating "safe sex." But the same educational system does not permit students to sing Christmas carols because the courts say it violates the First Amendment. Yet pornography, an $8 billion industry in America, is protected as freedom of speech!

It is no wonder God is still calling champions to take a stand. He looks for those with courage. The Lord will use *anybody* who will dare to walk with Him consistently. He commits Himself to those who take the challenge. What a thought—God Almighty making a pledge like that! Just look at this:

> No one will be able to stand up against you all the days of your life. As I was with Moses, so I will be with you; I will never leave you nor forsake you. Be strong and courageous, because you will lead these people to inherit the land I swore to their forefathers to give them. Be strong and very courageous. Be careful to obey all the law My servant Moses gave you; do not turn from it to the right or to the left, that you may be successful wherever you go. Do not let this Book of the Law depart from your mouth; meditate on it day and night, so that you may be

careful to do everything written in it. Then you will be prosperous and successful. Have I not commanded you? Be strong and courageous. Do not be terrified; do not be discouraged, for the Lord your God will be with you wherever you go.

Joshua 1:5-9

If that isn't a call for champions, I'm an astronaut. Let's look at this call piece by piece and see what's in it for today's potential champions.

Commitment

Often we make new commitments to the Lord at camps, in church, at mission conferences and at Christian concerts. Those times of public declaration are important, for they give us a chance to take a stand for God in front of others. What we find in this passage, however, is not an individual committing himself to the Lord, but the Lord making a commitment to someone. "As I was with Moses, so I will be with you."

If ever there was a champion that God stood with, it was Moses. Moses lived through the ten plagues, escaped from Pharaoh at the Red Sea, wandered for 40 years in the wilderness, put up with the grumbling of his people, and finally died at the edge of the Promised Land. The same Lord who promised to be with Moses promises to be with you, no matter what.

Think about that: the same Lord who spoke when there was nothing and all creation popped into existence makes that kind of pledge. The same Lord who stood with the prophets like Elijah, Elisha, Jeremiah, and Daniel says He will never leave you. The very God who calmed the storms, fed the thousands, healed the sick, raised the dead, and defeated hell and the demons promises to never, never, never, forsake you. Never! With that assurance, who wouldn't want to be God's champion?

Courage

There are many people in history who have been models of courage: Robert E. Lee, General MacArthur, Dwight D. Eisenhower, George Washington, Abraham Lincoln, Martin Luther, John Calvin, John and Charles Wesley, Madame Curie, Florence Nightingale, Joan of Arc, and Corrie Ten Boom, to name only a few. Despite the odds, they dared to take a stand that shook the world. The Lord issues a call for His people also to be courageous. In fact, He says it four times in Joshua 1, verses 6, 7, 9, and 18. He really means it.

Consistency

In Joshua 1:8, God calls all champions to a consistent time in His Word. He tells us, "Do not let this Book of the Law depart from your mouth, meditate on it day and night, so that you may be careful to do everything written in it." Without consistency, there is no fuel for power.

We sometimes say that a person who lives his life by consistent standards has integrity. Ted Engstrom tells a story about a judge who embraced a consistent lifestyle despite the howling of his opponents:

> A judge was campaigning for re-election. He had a reputation for integrity. He was a distinguished and honorable gentleman of no small charity. His opponent was conducting a vicious, mud-smearing, unfair campaign against him.
>
> Somebody approached the judge and asked, "Do you know what your opponent is saying

about you? Do you know he is criticizing you? How are you going to handle it? What are you going to do about it?" The judge looked at his counselors and his campaign committee and calmly replied, "Well, when I was a boy I had a dog. And every time the moon was full, that hound dog would howl and bark at the bright face of the moon. We never did sleep very well those nights. He would bark and howl at the moon all night." With that, the judge concluded his remarks.

"That's beside the point," his campaign manager impatiently said. "You've told us a nice story about your dog, but what are you going to do about your critic?"

The judge explained, "I just answered you! When the dog barked at the moon, the moon kept right on shining! I don't intend to do anything but keep right on shining, and I'll ignore the criticism, as the moon ignored the dog. I'll just keep on shining! Quietly, calmly, beautifully!"[1]

God calls His champions to a calm, consistent walk according to the Word. Despite the "howling" of society when an evangelist falls into sin and another scandal makes the headlines, the Lord still says to individuals, "Be strong and very courageous. Be careful to obey all the law my servant Moses gave you; do not turn from it to the right or to the left, that you may be successful wherever you go." Consistency is the key!

Only One
You may read this and think, "What difference can one person make, anyway?" Well, consider this:

God Is Still Calling Champions

- One vote gave America the English language instead of German.
- Thomas Jefferson and John Quincy Adams were elected President by one vote in the Electoral College.
- One vote changed France from a monarchy to a republic.
- One vote gave Adolf Hitler leadership of the Nazi party.
- One vote per precinct elected John Kennedy President of the United States.[2]

What if the following people had said things like this:

Billy Graham: "I'm only an evangelist. What can I do?"

Mother Teresa: "What difference can one nun make in all of India?"

Stephen Curtis Chapman: "Does the world need another Christian songwriter?"

James Dobson: "Do we really need another radio talk show?"

Chuck Swindoll: "How much of a difference can a Christian author make, anyway?"

Chuck Colson and Harold Morris: "Who needs to hear from a convict?"

The one who led you to Christ: "He/she has probably already heard the Gospel."

Because they refused to be captured by such negative thinking, these people made a difference. Each one cast his or her vote and became a champion for Christ.

The challenge of this book has been to motivate you to cast your "one vote" for things that will outlast you. There are a variety of things that campaign for that vote, but only one will last forever—the life that follows the Lord's way.

It takes guts to follow Him in all areas of your life. The call to be a champion God's way requires submission to authorities, moral purity, and a value system that honors the Lord in all areas. Walking in this lifestyle allows us to help those struggling with problems like abortion, true and false guilt, anger, and low self-esteem. Our strength comes from understanding the teaching of Scripture, a prayer life that has a punch to it, and the power of the Holy Spirit flowing through us. We protect ourselves from attack as we "suit up" according to Ephesians 6:10-19 and dance against the devil. When we make a decision for Christ, we stand above the crowd in the confidence of the Lord who said, "I will never leave you nor forsake you."

The world is waiting to see who dares to take God's challenge. The price isn't cheap, but one thing is for sure: I have never met anyone who, after casting his or her vote to be a champion for Christ, ever regretted it. That sure beats doing beer commercials.

Go for it!

Calling It Straight

1. In your opinion, why do we need champions today?

2. What characteristics should a champion have to meet the needs of our world today?

3. Can God instill in people today what former champions had given to them?

4. How are you going to cast *your* one vote? Have you thought of the consequences?

5. Will you also pray the prayer of champions?

Dear Lord,
   Please empower me to bring changes for the good in my world. May I have a passion for Your Holy Word, that my life may be spent, and my vote cast for the things that will last forever.

> Dedicated to Dancing Against the Devil

NOTES

Chapter one
1. A.W. Tozer, *The Pursuit of God*. Christian Publications, Camp Hill, Pa. 1948, p. 31.

Chapter two
1. Chuck Swindoll, *Come Before Winter... And Share My Hope*. Multnomah Press, Portland, Ore., 1985, pp. 161-62.

Chapter three
1. Bill Jones and Barry St. Clair, *Dating: Picking (and Being) A Winner*. San Bernardino: Here's Life Publishers, 1987, pp. 97-98.
2. *How to Help Your Child say "No" to Sexual Pressure*. Dallas: Word Publishing, p. 139.

Chapter four
1. The Peter's Brothers' "The Truth about Rock," cassette tapes, Rock Communications Group, St. Paul, Minn.

Chapter five
1. "Insights for Living." Newsletter, May 1987. Charles E. Swindoll, President.
2. C. Everett Koop. Cited in *One Church's Answer to Abortion* by Bill Hybels. Chicago: Moody Press, 1986, pp. 22-23.
3. Charles R. Swindoll, *Sanctity of Life: The Inescapable Issue*. Dallas: Word Publishing, 1990, p. 14.

Chapter six
1. The abbreviation of "The Tell-Tale Heart" taken from *Rebuilding Your Broken World*, by Gordon MacDonald, Atlanta: Oliver/Nelson Publishing, pp. 68-69.

Chapter seven
1. Tony Campolo, *Seven Deadly Sins*. Wheaton: Victor Books, 1987, pp. 59-60.

Chapter eight
1. Dr. James Dobson, *Hide or Seek*. Old Tappan, N.J.: Revell Publishers, 1974, pp. 17-19.
2. Dr. Charles Stanley, *Temptation*. Nashville: Oliver-Nelson Books, 1988, pp. 57-58.

Chapter nine
1. Josh McDowell, *More Than a Carpenter*. Wheaton: Tyndale House Publishing, 1977, p. 108.

Chapter ten
1. As quoted in *Dear Lord*, selected by Bill Adler Nashville, Tenn.: Thomas Nelson Publishing, 1982.

2. Quoted in *More Letters to God,* compiled by Eric Marshall and Stuart Hample. New York: Simon and Schuster, Essandess Special Editions, 1967.
3. The Atlanta *Journal*, Atlanta, Georgia, "Religion and the American Teenager" November 16, 1991, section E, page 6.
4. *Christianity Today,* "Cheers for Prayers," January 13, 1992, p. 44.
5. Terry Wardle, *One to One.* Camp Hill, Pa.: Christian Publications, Incorporated, 1989, p. 28.

Chapter eleven
1. Quoted in Fred Hartley, *100% Beyond Mediocrity.* Old Tappan, N.J.: Revell Company, 1983, p. 135.
2. Fred Hartley, *100% Beyond Mediocrity.* Old Tappan, N.J.: Revell Company, 1983, 136-7.
3. Fred Hartley, *100% Beyond Mediocrity.* Old Tappan, N.J.: Revell Company, 1983, p. 137.

Chapter thirteen
1. Ted W. Engstrom with Robert C. Carson, *Integrity.* Dallas: Word Publishers, 1987, p. 13.
2. Mel and Norma Gabler, *What Are They Teaching Our Children?* Wheaton: Victor Books, 1985, p. 13.